Acknowledgements

This book is dedicated to my family who have tolerated this strange obsession and at times have shared in the fun too. In gratitude for their patience.

Every attempt has been made to contact and consult owners about the content describing their cars but with changes of address and of ownership on a global basis this has not always been possible. The information produced is published in good faith and is believed to be correct and as accurate an account as the author understands with the data available at the time. If errors have appeared in connection with any particular car the author would be happy to be advised.

The High Peaks Trial 1934, AYK597, Dorothy Champney's Imp, as no 18, in action.
(Photo credit Mrs A.Gripper, from a collection by kind permission A.B.Demaus)

THE RILEY IMP

HISTORIES AND PROFILES

BY
JOHN GATHERCOLE

A recent photo by Noel Wyatt of the Imp - Chassis No 6025503

Wisteria Cottage Publishing Ltd

First Published July 2008 by Wisteria Cottage Publishing Ltd
Minor revision August 2008

ISBN 978-0-9953559-1-2

Printed by
Worcester City Digital
Worcester
WR1 3AU

Useful contacts:
The Riley Register
Mrs Doreen Ager, Membership Secretary
8 chapel road
Great Totham
Malden, CM9 8DA

Or visit the website www.rileyregister.com

The Riley Motor Club
PO Box 166
Andover
SP11 0TP

Or visit the website www.rileymotorclub.org

Front Cover Photo by Ian Stainburn. BYY575 on a very wet Inter Register Rally, Hereford, 1992
Rear Cover Photo by Mark Ballard. AVR 718 Ulster Imp in action at Prescott Hill Climb 2002

Foreword

This book represents part of John's life. For many years he has maintained records about every aspect of Imp production and their subsequent ownership on a global basis. Three years ago I was at Lime Rock where I saw two beautiful Imps. For many years I saw my cousin Rosalind's Imp in Australia, (Percy Riley's youngest daughter).

I found the book fascinating and could not stop reading the contents until I reached the end. The Riley Register Committee have taken another successful step in their Riley model series.

The book has evoked many memories of my Mother's tales regarding her Imp, which I remember being shut away in our garage at the outbreak of World War II. However what today would be called industrial politics intervened during the war, when the Chairman of Bristol Aeroplane Co. persuaded my Father to part with the Imp for his son's 21st birthday present. Rileys made the Beaufighter undercarriage!

My Mother would be delighted to know that her Imp is in John's book, which I commend to all Riley enthusiasts

Victor Riley

Table of Contents

Willy Oosten (Imp in '9' form), en route to success in the 1950 Rallye Evian Mont Blanc

Introduction

The Riley Imp is often said to deserve a place among the finest looking sports cars. This book is an attempt to list them, whether surviving or lost for good, as produced during the years 1934 and 1935. Having maintained an unofficial register of these cars for some 35 years, the process of updating and keeping track of Imp movements never ends and there comes a time to publish and.... the rest. So despite all that effort, this book remains little more than a snapshot and carries all of those limitations. At least a bench mark has been provided and others can then carry on the process. This is necessary as "new" Imps with uncertain pedigree have a habit of appearing so this exercise is useful in that sense. Of course 'copiers' of these fine cars are given additional knowledge to help them on their way! But to draw all this out into the light of day is a preferred route and can therefore assist the Riley Register in its prime task of being the arbiter in matters of progeny and authenticity.

All this started with the work of Tim Dyke, during his ownership of both an MPH and an Imp and who began listing known Imps in about 1971, I taking it forward in 1973 at the suggestion of Nev and Barbara Farquhar. That said, my own interest in the breed began with my purchase of BYY575 in 1962. Then, as a curate in Durham it was my sole transport and at times had to ferry my non-driving vicar on longer excursions. Since then, it has served as honeymoon transport, has competed in speed events, rallies and driving tests and enjoyed a great deal of largely trouble free continental touring. The contributions of others to this book must also be acknowledged and grateful thanks are due to so many, besides Tim Dyke, including the encouragement of the Riley Register, help from the Riley Motor Club and use of the resources and photos from the Riley Record, special mention being made of Victor Riley (Jnr) himself. Add to that, Peter Banner, Vernon Barker, Chris Buck, Robin Cameron, Jim Cartwright, Tim Ely, Rodney Green, Nev and Barbara Farquhar, Ian Hall, Tony Irwin, Alan Lomas, Mike McQuire, Gordon Middleton, Henrik Schou-Nielsen, Imp owners around the globe and others. The cars in Australia are a special group, and histories are very difficult to resolve but a number of enthusiasts there have been a great help including Phil Evans, Ean McDowell, Brian Mole and Noel Wyatt. Phil Irwin assisted with some UK registration conundrums. Some specific histories came from Arnold Farrar prior to his death and who then held works sales registers and he was happy to share that information.

An exercise of this sort carries a number of limitations. Firstly, despite there being little more than an 18 months production period there is no distinctive listing as Imp chassis numbers run integrally with all other production 'Nines'. The cars were assembled in the Competition Department at the Riley Works at Durbar Avenue, Coventry in small batches, some probably to individual order. The flow of their chassis numbers is commentary on this as pairs and trios of cars appear in the general listings. If gearbox and rear axle numbers were generally available, they might show the batch pattern in which parts were drawn forward for assembly, not being in numerical sequence. Secondly, the company's records were lost in the blitz in WWII when Coventry suffered terribly and the factory was heavily damaged. As a result of this the tracing of Imps presents something of a problem,

1

and at times we may be clutching at straws. Gaps in the overall chassis number sequences, working from today's assembled lists, may imply loss as of any of the many models the company were at that time trying to sustain, which led in part to its own undoing. However the reverse argument also holds that the lists which follow must represent the vast bulk of the Imps produced. Two factors apply. The first is that these are durable motor cars. The level of engineering excellence (some would say they are over engineered), has meant that the survival rate is pretty high. The second factor is that these are highly memorable motor cars. The tracing of histories is shot through with occasions of, "there used to be one stored in a barn over at…" and "We regularly saw that car…" and more. Details of colour, parts of registrations, distinguishing features, all seem to have stuck in someone's memory somewhere and the same is true of the demise of cars which are known to have gone missing for one reason or another. So, within the corporate and international memory of keepers and users down the years we must be getting fairly close to the facts. 115 cars are listed here including a few duplications. We shall never know the total produced but this may not be far out, bearing in mind that only 50 Sprites were made, and about 14 MPHs. The third surprising feature of the exercise is that they still do turn up having been thought to be gone for good. As a result, this listing of chassis numbers and details as verified, probably amounts to as extensive a record as is possible of the numbers actually produced. They were made in small batches, probably to order and with detailed differences as requested.

The photos used throughout the book deserve an explanation They are mixed bag being taken on a variety of cameras, gathering information over a period of now nearly 40 years. Poor quality was however felt of lesser importance than the telling of the story. Others have given permission for their own material to be used, for which I am hugely grateful and I have tried to give acknowledgements and to honour copyright wherever I can. The origins of some photos however remain untraceable despite a range of efforts and this is to be regretted. Gratitude remains however for their addition to the value of the overall story.

Special thanks are due to Peter Banner for his work on Coventry City's registrations, to Conway Hall, Ian Hall and Alan Lomas for both technical and textual proof reading and to Victor Riley for providing his kind Foreword.

John Gathercole
2008

The successful 1934 team of Riley Imps for the RSAC Scottish Rally, left to right Dorothy Champney and Kay Petre, in AYK597, Edgar Maclure and Eddie Maher in KV 8932, T.C.Griffiths and Bill Greenaway in KV 8025. C.A.Richardson in KV 8933, A.J.Dickson is in the MPH, KV5694.
(A Riley Record Photograph)

2

1- The Prototype

The prototype Imp for the 1933 Show. The Riley Record, by kind permission.

It was at the October Motor show at Olympia in 1933 that the new Imp was first presented. Its sporting pedigree was plain to see at that stage, succeeding, as it did, the Gamecock and in closed form, the Lincock, the latter with its seating layout as a 2+2. The Imp can be seen as a direct successor to the Brooklands, only if the shift in contemporary sports car design is pushed to the limit. Admittedly, the Ulster Imp, not announced till months later, did try to take up some of that sporting tradition. The Brooklands had ceased production in 1931, the Gamecock ran in 1932 so the continuation of the pedigree had to be addressed. However this new model on the '33 Stand was in Mendip Blue with matching upholstery, (as were all the show cars that year), a 2/4 seater with Triplex glass, speedometer, clock, licence holder, spring gaiters, screen wiper, driving mirror, rear tank, hood, price as complete £298. No fuel filler is visible and tank space limited with twin spares tucked in hard against the rear panel and seat squab, according to the artist's drawing of the car (above) as intended. These days, the car on the stand would probably be regarded as a design exercise. At that point, for Riley's it was a statement of intent.

The Autocar in its issue of September 22 1933 wrote: *The family tree of the Riley marque does however display a new branch, for there is to be an extra type to that most successful car, the Riley Nine. The additional type is to be called the 'Imp'. It follows the same mechanical specification as the Nine, but has a shorter wheelbase of 7'6" and carries a light occasional 4 seater open touring body. The engine is of the special series type with 2 carburetters and a high compression ratio, and the car is definitely intended to have an extra 'snappy' road performance. The price will be £298.*

The fact that the car was a mock up with vital ingredients missing at this stage was not unusual in such times. Even Bentleys were known bring forward a new model where the timing of the Motor Show did not fit entirely with the development side of the programme! What remains a puzzle is the transition from the Imp as displayed in October 1933 and the very different car which emerged for the Scottish Rally in the Spring of 1934. The car by then had gained a fuel filler cap and lost its

3

Julian Majzub's Brooklands - fully road equipped but still Spartan.

occasional rear seats but with rakish lines had more importantly been transformed from the rather obvious poor relation to its Gamecock predecessor to a sporting motor which continues to this day to be a real eye catcher, park it where so ever you will. As part of the shift in sports car design in the mid thirties, as presented, this new model is in part a comment on what was happening in that period. The appeal of the more basic and rugged designs exemplified in the Brooklands, was giving way to more comfort and refinement.

There was also a shift to meet the demands of the wider car market, where bulk production was requiring the meeting of more general needs and therefore greater compromise was being sought. There was in general a demand for family cars offering brisk performance and the specialist car makers were moving more into the luxury sector and away from sports cars as the Vintage years had understood and known them. This trend was not limited to the UK: the same could be seen in France and Italy. Against these odds, many of the greater names of sports car producers were fast disappearing and the more comfortable cars were becoming heavier and more ponderous. While engine development proceeded, chassis design had tended to mark time, while bodies grew heavier. At the same time in the field of motor sport, pure racing and speed events were becoming much more specialised and less accessible to the enthusiastic amateur and were giving way at the popular level to trials and speed testing. So the growth in trials and sporting tests was keeping the popular sports car market going but in a new direction, This was having its own influence on the production of more rigid (and in the case of Riley's) heavier chassis frames, and was demanding cars with lower gearing while top speed was becoming less important than 'getaway' as befitted these more accessible forms

4

The chassis of the prototype with All Helical gearbox. Featured in The Riley Record.

of motor sport. Thus, the new market now to be served required aero screens, quick fill caps and the overall sporting appearance of a car that could perform well in club events while still offering a more refined overall motoring experience.

For this new Imp, the development of the chassis had mainly taken place in 1933. The car shown in October at Olympia possessed a dropped frame, under slung at the rear, with a deep centre section of five and a half inches in the side members - a radical departure from Riley's tradition of a light and whippy chassis, now presenting a rigid cross-braced sloping platform on which the newly designed lower body would sit. This configuration was in line with the now proven under slung racing six cylinder cars prepared for the September 1933 Tourist Trophy, also known as the Grebe. (See picture p.8). Perhaps on those grounds the Company was able to claim that the yet unproven Imp was to be :

"a genuine sports car, capable of holding the road like a leech, possessing clean sporting lines, with a performance which makes it outstanding among its fellows."
(Riley Record Sept 1933)

This first prototype chassis, if heavier, was not yet boxed on its inner faces based on Riley's long standing use of the open channel section framing. That comes later. At least one open framed chassis exists today (see notes on chassis no. 6026133) and is unique in that respect. This important car will be described in the section dealing with specific cars. In 1933 the range of contemporary nine horsepower models did not have a boxed chassis and it was only later in the Spring of 1934 that the fully boxed chassis emerged for the Imp, but not for the MPH.

Fitted for the Show car was an all helical gearbox, larger brakes, centre lock wheels and the Brooklands/vintage bronze control levers for hand throttle and advance and retard mechanism at the centre boss of the steering column around the horn button, these having lapsed with the demise of the Brooklands model. This reintroduction was a departure from the contemporary set up applying to the other 1933 models

Derek Holloway's 1933 March Special compares with the1933 Imp Show car

including the now discontinued Gamecock and the Lynx '9' 2-door, still in production at this stage.

The effect of the new chassis layout gave the car a more sporting line and the driver has the sense of sitting lower and between the rear wheels on the short wheelbase. The appearance in profile is a departure from the earlier types including the sporting models in the Riley portfolio. The line is enhanced by the set of the small sloping radiator sitting just to the rear of the front axle line, a point of styling as well as of engineering of some importance for sports cars of the day.

The bodywork of this prototype Show car borrows from the 2 door Lynx of the time, but perhaps even more from the March Special. The Earl of March had designed a 2/4 seater on the Nine chassis with long flowing wings, upswept scuttle and cut away doors. On the Imp prototype, the set of the forward hinged doors, the raised scuttles, the full screen with fold flat mechanism and the twin spares were followed, but knock on wheels had arrived appearing as they did on some later two door Lynx models and the post prototype Grebe, (the first of these having six stud wheels). Like the Lynx and the March, the show car had bucket front seats, as the *Autocar* picture on page 7 shows. The wings were of the full flow style, in a single span incorporating the running board with rounded or rolled edges but lacking the dropped valance midway along the front wings such as occurs on other models of that year. The rear wings had a full drop to the rear, tapering away rather as on the March Special but carrying forward the lines of the front wings. The bonnet had its louvres cut to a diamond pattern, as was standard practice on models in 1933. An external hood was to be fitted, with pram irons, if the artist's drawing was followed through as the show car suggests it was.

That is where this chapter ends. The first production Imp to appear on the road was in March of 1934, when it emerged in different guise.

6

The prototype Imp as presented in 'Mendip blue', as were all Rileys at the 1933 October motor show. (Autocar photo with permission of LAT Photographic)[1]

2 – The New Imp

On the 7th April 1934, two Imps were registered, as KV8025 and KV8026, respectively chassis numbers 602449 and 602450. The long winter months had seen a substantial reworking of the October show car recipe and the emerging car was of a different order. The parallel with the emergence of the MPH is of course of great importance. The bodies were built by Allan Riley's branch of the business, Midland Motor Bodies. Allan had a love of design and according to Victor (Jnr) was forever sketching out developing ideas and schemes, though the shift in styling arguably may include another element which is explained later.

The appearance of the six cylinder big sister was a month before the first Imp, in the 1934 RAC Rally on March 13th when two prototype MPHs appeared. Starting from Glasgow, the MPH, KV 6079, was driven by Rupert Riley and Ann Gibson Watt, the other KV 5694, by A.W.Von Der Becke, (Motor Sept 4 '34). Both of these MPH cars had run in the 1933 TT as 'Racing Sixes' in 'Grebe' form. Now re-bodied and re-worked and apart from the rear cover hiding the spare wheel, the MPH design paired with the Imp in most details. Specifically, the body 'tub' is of the same dimensions[2] and the flared wings to the front and the chopped off rears are shared, apart from the need for an overall 6" extra amidships to accommodate the six cylinder engine. In the literature, early MPH cars were also offered with the same gearbox recipe as the Imp, of either the All-Helical manual box, or the Wilson ('self change') 'Preselecta', (this in place of the Armstrong Siddeley box as fitted

---

[1] This car, as KV 8026 took part in a 1934 Rally with 28 other Nines, according to A.T. Birmingham, 'Pre 1939 Riley Motorcars', op cit p 166, 2nd Edition. See notes on Chassis no 6024450 in the listing in section 9

[2] see page 11

The 1933 TT 'Grebe' prepared for Staniland, (photo © by kindness of Mrs M Martin)

eventually). As to whose styling was the formative, it can be argued that the Imp was the test bed for this new turn of events in the Riley family. There was no sporting six cylinder car at the 1933 show, while the 'mocked up' nature of the Imp prototype might indicate the development programme was centred on the highly effective Nine engine to which the company was strongly committed in 1933.

The Riley Grebe has to have its place in the development of the Imp. Some of the new Imp chassis features were directly adopted as already mentioned and while there may be 'no substitute for litres', one might argue that the balanced design of the Imp was essentially laid down in the autumn of 1933 in part using this as the driving force. The argument has also been put that the MPH looks like a stretched Imp where the Imp does not look like a shrunken MPH! The Imp is often referred to as among the best balanced and prettiest sports car designs built. But whatever the arguments, the winter of 1933/4 saw an evolution into this classic design.

Opportunity existed for a small sports car to fit into the popular 1100c.c. category and in which there was a lively sporting market, which MG were exploiting but in which a vacuum existed for a quality car. Wolseley were developing the Hornet and in 1933 presented their 1271c.c. engine with twin carburetters, oil cooler and remote control 4 -speed gearbox. The 1933 Singer Nine sports 4-seater had a top speed of 65mph, with its slab tank, cycle wings and raised scuttles. In 1934 Triumph were working on the exciting Dolomite but this was to be a 2-litre straight eight twin overhead cam project due to appear in only small numbers a little later.

But this reference to Triumph is significant. Donald Healey had joined Riley for a short period. Convinced of the potency of the 'Nine' engine and its six cylinder associate, he had had opportunity, courted by Victor Riley, to drive for Rileys in competition and by 1933 he was:

8

"covering 20,000 miles a year in international rallies and trials as well as many lesser events at home in cars based on the standard product, though modified in many small respects."[3]

He describes in his autobiography, the challenges of the Automobilclub von Deutchland in 1931 mostly over roads that were not really roads at all...

"some stretches in the Balkans down into Yugoslavia where the cars were given a terrible bashing which of course, was excellent as a proving ground for the manufacturers."[4]

Healey joined the Riley company at the invitation of Victor to help prepare a team of cars for the 1933 Alpine Rally. He was particularly taken with the Lynx Tourer,

"a very snappy little car with the 9hp engine which, thanks to its hemispherical head and short, light pushrods operated by camshafts halfway up the cylinder block, was capable of quite high revs and, in standard form, would push the car along at around 75 mph. It was an extremely good car that was capable of putting up high speeds on Alpine tests. I spent some weeks getting the cars ready at the factory; four were prepared – a team of three plus a spare. When the 1933 Alpine Rally came along they justified our faith in them, two of us winning Glacier Cups, myself in the Brooklands and Victor Leverett with one of the Lynxes."[5]

For him this drive in the Brooklands was the "least comfortable" event he ever tackled in pursuit of chassis improvement. Despite that:

"While I worked for (Rileys), I chose events where the degree of engine tuning required was small, but where a fairly considerable amount of work was essential on the chassis and running gear to make cars suitable for the big international trials and rallies."[6]

Despite his contribution to improving the rugged handling of the breed, Healey was however uncertain about over-committing himself to Rileys long term,

"the four brothers, each a well qualified specialist in his own particular aspect of car manufacture... able to design an excellent car and even produce it and sell it at a price that was competitive with the products of the big manufacturers, - they were good designers, good entrepreneurs – but not good accountants!"[7]

To him, the cars were 'too good value for money', he wondered how long they would keep going. But for our purpose he was with Rileys into that crucial winter of 1933/4 when the Imp's longer term design was being forged.

---

[3] 'My world of cars', by Peter Garnier with Brian Healey, pub Patrick Stephens Ltd. page 57.
[4] op cit page57
[5] op cit p.57
[6] op cit p 56
[7] op cit p 54ff

Donald Healey in the prototype Triumph Dolomite 8 in 1934 at Perranporth
(photo by kind permission Brian Healey)

At that point Healey was courted by Colonel Holbrook, Managing Director of Triumph who was looking to build a car to compete with the Riley Nine. Healey had driven the Seven and the Super Seven in events but warned Holbrook that if the proposed Gloria were to compete with Riley someone "with sufficient experience would be required on their payroll". With a brief, but grateful, look back at Rileys in that winter, Healey was appointed Experimental Manager to work at Triumph with Charles Ridley. We do not know what part he played in the reworking of the Imp and the emergence of the MPH, but his presence at Rileys, with his formidable trials and rally experience and his interest in design and development while these were being re-conceived is a fact. And a look at the fine lines of the 1935 Triumph Dolomite 8 in relation to emerging Riley products (see p 48), may speak for itself.

In its revised form, and on its 7' 6" wheelbase, the more rugged body of the 1934 production Imp had lost its rolled edge wings, which now fold over a neat but stronger valance that is wrapped into the wing edge and has a turned finish at its lower lip. Because of their span some cars, but not all, have front wings fitted with a supporting spar half way down their length to minimise vibration and these were mounted on the chassis side, with retaining rivets into the wing panel and also into the valance. Interestingly a few Imps produced did have the rolled wing shape including chassis no 6026133. The rear wings as already noted, in sharp contrast to the show car give a chopped off look to the tail end, exposing the rear wheels but adding to the whole a purposeful and forward look. The wings are broken by a separate running board to which they are bolted front and rear. In turn these are mounted on two substantial side members protruding from the chassis frame. Gone are the raised scuttles to give a smoothed line gently building to a point towards the cockpit rear and a redesigned low fold flat screen, departing from Riley's previous fittings, is supplemented by two removable but rigidly mounted aero screens which can be stowed in specially designed sleeves in the lids above the scuttle tool boxes. (See photos pp 77, 113,134 159 &164). The occasional rear seat has gone and the dished rear body panel, now housing the spare wheel slopes at a 45 degree angle, forward of which sits the large 12 gallon fuel tank hidden between the sides of the rear body panels. The spare is mounted on a central shaft which protrudes through the removable rear cover from a heavy 'A' frame which locks the rear of the body to a round rear-of-chassis cross member so providing a rigid mounting point – a significant improvement on the hanging of the full weight of the spare wheel on the boot lid on other contemporary Rileys! Comparison with the body of the MPH is revealing. The only measurement that significantly differs is that of the bowed cross member at the cockpit rear. This rises to a central point about 3" higher than that on the Imp and continues the upward sweep of the distinctive rear panel fitted to the larger car. Otherwise the two bodies share the same measurements throughout both in width and depth.[8]

3 - Riley Imps: A Technical Description

The Imp uses the classic Riley format with engine and gearbox in semi floating unit, with a bearer bar on trunnions passing through the block while the rear gearbox neck fits into a formed rubber collar enclosed in a bronze casting mounted on to and above a chassis cross member. This is just forwards of a ball joint housing a universal joint allowing torque tube movement in unit with the rear axle, located to the chassis by the rear springs.[9] The cable brake system is centred in an assembly (including cable adjusters), mounted on the collar at the rear of the gear box, and incorporates the handbrake. There is no rigid chassis mounting here.

Innovations are external oil feeds to the rocker boxes at the front of the block and the appearance for the first time of round rocker boxes which seal better than their square predecessors, even if they make tappet adjustment more awkward! Both features were forerunners for the Merlin series engine to follow, though this engine was never originally fitted to the Imp. But among the chief of the Imp's special technical features are its cylinder head and its camshaft timing. Rare these days, the head (part number 9E 686), has improved compression with smaller hemispherical combustion chambers than the standard Nine being $2 \, ^9/_{32}$" diameter in the Imp as against the standard $2 \, ^3/_8$". No special pistons are listed for the standard Imp, the special head providing its distinctive boost.

Camshaft timing on the standard Imp has become a model for any who would improve performance. Two exhaust form camshafts are used as standard equipment. The exhaust cam carries a forward extension to drive the fan pulley as fitted to the sports models of earlier Nine development. The inlet cam, also using an exhaust profile, is fitted with the rev counter drive at its rear – a slotted tube insert. The cams are fully floating held in check by thrust bearings at the forward end. In the case of the inlet cam a small ball race and spring and pad is set in a blind bearing cap. The exhaust cam is held in check by a collar with four small springs acting on the front face of the camshaft thrust bearing, again taking forward thrust together with an oil seal. The cam gears are the later cast dished variety.

Using exhaust form cams extends considerably the standard valve overlap from 30° to a maximum of 62°. The inlet valve on the standard engine opens at top dead

---

[8] I am grateful to have compared the Imp and MPH cars of Ivor Halbert for these details

[9] See lower illustration on page 139 taken during Noel Wyatt's extensive restoration

centre (tdc), and closes 50° after bottom dead centre (abdc) with maximum lift at 115°. This gives a dwell of 230°. The exhaust opens 55° before bottom dead centre, and closes 30° after top dead centre giving a dwell of 265° with maximum opening at 102°. The use of two exhaust cams provides a much extended period of overlap, with the inlet opening 32° btdc[10] and closing at 53° abdc. To achieve this timing the inlet gear must be advanced one tooth bringing about this overlap. Double valve springs are used. One hazard found in engine assembly is the variation in the positioning of the crankshaft pinion keyway making precision setting difficult. Remarkably, this is not always consistent with TDC. To provide for this some have had to resort to the fitting of a stepped key which engineers will argue about with some heat, though there are not too many tales of breakages where components are fitted correctly! With this variation, the above figures may differ from engine to engine. The standard Nine set up used Coil and Distributor but the Special Series engine was offered with Scintilla Magneto ignition and fan assisted thermo siphon cooling. No special exhaust manifold was offered, the standard 'hotspot' type being used in the case of the Imp with a Vortex[11] silencer mounted under the nearside running board, with front and rear pipes offered additionally with a fishtail finish[12].

In the course of the development of the Riley '9' engine, lubrication of camshaft front bushes takes a number of forms, and the types are clearly visible when dismantled. The early cars had a feed pipe running from the centre of the upper face of the timing chest in a Y form to the front faces of the rocker boxes. Next came a fully internal feed through the cylinder head to the upper gallery inside the rocker box to the cam bearings. As already stated, from 1934 and Imp chassis no 6024449, oil-ways within the block were closed off and an external feed from the offside front of the block to the banjo unions on the front of each of the rocker boxes was fitted to give pressurised feed to the rocker gear. This modification applies generally on the Nine from chassis no 6027000 but was introduced on the Imp from its inception. The feeds to the large camshaft bearings differ in type, and the model types are not therefore interchangeable as it might appear at first glance. Damage will occur if the drip feed type is linked with the two hole bearing variety in which case oil will pass through without doing its lubrication work! The Imp is fitted with pressurised feed from the side of the block which must be coupled with the appropriate type of cam bearings.

The crankshaft used in the Imp conforms to the type size for the period. That is with an enlarged big end size of $1^{11}/_{16}$ " from the previous size of $1^9/_{16}$" after chassis no 6019800. The main bearings continue throughout the range at $1\frac{1}{2}$" front and rear.

After chassis no 6027900 and the commencement of the Merlin series, the big ends are enlarged to $1^7/_8$" while the rear main is enlarged from $1\frac{1}{2}$" to $1^5/_8$". Interesting

---

[10] Timing on BYY 575. But J.A.Robson, 'The Riley Nine Manual' published by Motor Racing Publications quotes 25°, p 91.

[11] "Tuning the Riley" A.F.Ashby - Brooklands Books- Gold Portfolio p.153 Spotted by Alan Lomas, to whom I am indebted, and who has the remains of one of these silencers.

[12] Offered in Sales and Service Bulletin, p 115 The Riley Motor Company. See also photo p143 below.

Imp frame during Peter Robert's restoration of 6027432, viewed from the rear

studies, quoted by Gordon Middleton, have shown the middle range of crank size to be the more vulnerable to breakage at certain speeds, notably around the 3000 to 3500 point, the earlier crank providing more resilience by its apparent flexibility! The Merlin crank is more robust and many owners have fitted these but with success only when care is taken in the enlargement of the receiving rebate in the rear section of the timing chest! One error encountered allowed the crankcase to vent freely to atmosphere! The Merlin crank has a shorter connecting rod with a higher piston crown giving a standard compression of 6.6:1 and can be fitted to good effect. The scarcity of these parts however means that many owners have sought alternative cranks and rods from modern suppliers. Some cars as will be seen in the listing that follows are now fitted with a full Merlin block including its oil filter and differing oil pump. The racing crank was fitted as standard to the Ulster Imps and to certain early Imps used in promotional and competitive work. Gordon Middleton points out that blocks had been gradually strengthened during the development of the Nine, the Merlin block finally having thicker walls and a more substantial housing for the rear main bearing but lacking the extra strengthening webs of the competition block's rear main bearing housing.

The whole car is built upon a substantial frame, constructed from $^1/_8$" thick steel plate, reinforced by diagonal channel bracing and tubular cross members. Fully boxed side members, 5½" deep at their centre section and widest point in line with the seats, these side members taper forwards to the dumb irons and rearwards, beneath the 'under-slung' rear axle to a full width tubular cross member into which the rear spring pins are mounted. The whole frame is boxed on its inner faces, panels substantially welded in top and bottom, variously described as either apprentice or Friday night welding due to its character! Large tubular cross members are riveted to the outer face of the frame passing through the inner added panels. Riveting, not bolting, was the method used to secure the cross members and also the associated

Chassis inner face showing boxing method and welding standard, (photo AVR718)

chassis components.[13] The front springs contain seven leaves, lying under at their forward end and rolling over at their rear on an offset inboard mounting, below and behind the engine mounting plate. With the chassis taper, their fronts are outboard while the rears are inboard of the frame line. The rear springs have nine leaves and are 34" between centres. These roll over at their forward end and under at the rear end, providing support in the sprung roll. Bi-metal cast brake drums of 15" are fitted. On the Ulster, the springs have forged eyes, changing slightly the level of setting.

Imps were first offered at £295 according to the introductory sales brochure with the All Helical gearbox. These were only taken in small numbers. The gear ratios were quoted as 20.86, 13.5, 8.06, and 5.5 final drive. The box is stated to have all gears "of a helical pattern giving four silent speeds". The Ulster Imp was similarly announced at £450 with a gearbox, "with direct drive in top and third speed gear wheels in constant mesh and have helical tooth form to ensure silent running and easy gear change" – plainly the Silent 3rd box was intended here. In the event more popular and perhaps fashionable was the fitting of the Wilson ENV Type 75 high ratio 'preselelecta' gearbox for the Imp range, stamped 'HR' after the serial number, driving through a 1st or 2nd Type centrifugal clutch (used up to chassis no 6027686). Total cost £325. Arnold Farrar's figures for this box are 3.89, 2.22, 1.46 and 1, with the 5.25 rear axle. Regarding final drives, Rileys are often criticised for their low ratios and the search for something higher which will still pull the car is often debated. 5.25 was the provided ratio for Imps and "IMP 5.25" is stamped on the rear axle casing locking plate, while the Ulster was originally fitted with 5:1. Riley's publicity originally quoted a 5.5 rear axle for the Imp and 4.77 for the Ulster Imp (manual box). The Imp is quite a heavy car, at 17 cwt while the Ulster Imp is under 14cwt.

---

[13] Riley Record, May 1936 reproduced in the Riley Register Bulletin March 2007, p 13.

With the chassis lying at a different angle to the transmission to that of the standard cars, the Imp like other sports models is under slung and the ride height for the engine differs. The engine bearer bar is held in bushed mountings set in a special hollow casting, common also to the six cylinder cars, which bolts directly onto chassis mounting plates. The casting is hollow up to the waistline and has a split bronze liner. From base of the casting to centre line of the bearer bar is 2″ and the height from chassis plate face to base of bolt head seating is 3″. The bar on the Imp is sturdier than the standard car – 1″ diameter at its outboard ends, the centre section between the threading is 1.125″. The mounting bolts themselves are 4.125″ overall length, and threaded $^7/_{16}$″ BSF. Mounting cones and rubbers differ accordingly.

Inside, the single rear seat squab had a thin cushioning surround and a central panel separating the two seat backs and square 'float-on-air' cushions lay either side of the transmission tunnel which hid the torque tube transmission. (see p.97). Instrumentation appears to consist of, from left to right, a British Jaeger 2 ½″ clock, an oil pressure gauge above a fuel Hobson Telegauge, a large rev counter, an ammeter above magneto switch, starter button, panel lighting, and ignition pull switches, and a speedometer, (though there seems much inconsistency). A temperature gauge was not fitted as original equipment and some cars are fitted with Andre Hartford Telecontrol dampers with the associated gauge or gauges. Two helmet type panel lamps were fitted. Clock, rev counter and speedometer are all British Jaeger. The original headlamp equipment mounted on 6″ stems was the Rotax KL 590/7. Some cars have K 590/7 fitted. The package in finished form met the requirement of the international class G for competition purposes[14]. Chassis numbers are stamped in the front face of the nearside dumb iron, vulnerable in any shunt, (see illus p.65), but may be found elsewhere- e.g. on the outer face of that member and were also provided on a diamond shaped bulkhead plate.

4 - The Competition Imps and the Ulster Imp.

At the Company's initiative, Imps took their share in competitive events and made their mark. 'Works' activity was short lived with the rapidly changing face of the Sport and the arrival of the 1½ litre Sprite. But over the years a number of successful racing drivers started their careers in Imps, and plenty of the cars listed in this book have competitive history in their pedigree. But Company policy meant that they built particular characteristics and features into their own competition cars, effectively creating a class within the generic Imp family.

While the term 'Ulster', is often applied to the competition Imps, and especially those with the boat tailed body, the name is used ambiguously, perhaps intentionally. At Le Mans in 1934 Rileys entered one car in near standard trim, driven by the ladies Dorothy Champney and Kay Petre, and two others described as "specially bodied Imps", namely KV9475 and KV9476. More of these were prepared for the Ards TT in the September of that year, and the name "Ulster" is usually applied to these cars. But, to confuse, the sales brochure of both the standard

---

[14] <u>Motor</u> Sept 4, 1934

The 'Ulster' Chassis frame of AVR 718 after cleaning. Note the fuel tank mounting bar and its locating slot. Front spring mountings are aligned with the forward cross member.

car and that of the Ulster Imp carried pictures of the road trimmed Imp KV8025. The dating of the publicity brochures would be a fine prize and might indicate what was in the Company's mind. There is no doubt from photos that the three cars entered in the Scottish Rally in June, and the Le Mans Cars (AYK 597 competed in both events), had full competition mechanics, as did certain others.

The matter of the naming is confused further by the specifications listed in the Company's own publicity. While the photographs on brochures for both the standard and Ulster Imps is identical – KV 8025 - the listed specifications differ. Thus the Imp is described as having a 'preselectagear' with column control and automatic clutch and sells at £325. The Ulster - selling at £450 - is described as having the All Helical manual gearbox and manual single plate clutch (as originally presented at the 1933 Motor Show). But the Ulsters, as they later became known, running both at Le Mans and in the TT, were fitted with the ENV box. The engine was given special pistons with 1 ½ mm rings and a gudgeon pin of $^5/_8''$ diameter and the big crankshaft with detachable balance weights and pumped cooling.

Here, it is worthwhile to describe in detail the main features of the Ulster, as it emerged and became known as the cars that ran in the 1934 TT or were among the few others of like design. The source of a good deal of this uses the opportunity to draw on AVR 718 studied in relation to other Ulsters, as it remains the most original example of these cars, having had a fairly light competition life, compared with its fellows and therefore having suffered the least amount of alteration and development. So it is helpful to offer some notes on the frame, the mechanical set up and the body of the racing Ulster Imp as it emerged.

The frame itself follows the form of the standard Imp, fully boxed, welded and riveted, with two main differences. The TT cars carried a large oval tank mounted on a cradle on an additional cross member and held in place by two large spring steel straps with double threaded tie bolts. This cross member is let into the inner

16

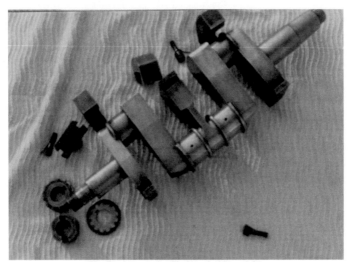

The Racing crank with detachable weights

faces of the frame in two specially provided locating slots and retained by bolts. The other more significant difference is the forward mounting of the front springs. While on the standard car the front spring mounting pins are located about an inch higher than the centre line of the front cross member linking the dumb irons, the Ulster version has the spring mounting pin aligned with the cross member itself. This both re-sets the lie of the spring and has some effect on castor angle. (This also features on the MPH frame). Both differences are visible in the photo on page 16 of the frame of AVR718 after cleaning[15]. Some of the visible holes in the frame are original, others are attempts by Hugh Cocker, the second owner, to lighten and lose metal. He confessed, having put much effort into these mods, that compensatory beer drinking put the equivalent amount of weight on around his waist!

The mechanical differences are more extensive. This group of cars used features Riley had developed in competition with some interesting additions. The engine block is mounted on a more substantial bearer bar and its cones and has seven webs to strengthen the rear main bearing mount in place of the normal five. The racing crank is fully machined but carries large detachable balance weights, with a front bearing of 1½" and rear main of 1¾". The big end journals are $1\,{}^{31}/_{32}$". The large detachable weights are retained in place on tapered slides with retaining bolts and split pins all to be removed before the crank may be withdrawn from the block. Re-assembly means these weights can only be fitted once the crank is in the block. Oil is supplied from a much finned 14 pint electron sump through unique manifolding, (see p.18 & 68-9) to a triple plunger pump driven by three eccentrics from the rear of the idler gear giving hot oil pressure of 75 psi, according to a letter in 1935 from

---

[15] compare photos pp 49, 60, 65 (upper), 103 (upper), (Ulsters) & 140,142 and 171 (standard).

Triple plunger oil pump feed arrangements

Rupert Riley. The 'works' cars appear to have been fitted with a sub sump, but not the private entrants. An external feed provides oil to the rockers as for the standard car and round covers, introduced for the first time, are fitted to the rocker boxes. The rockers fitted were 'KE805' type and additionally machined to lighten them as are their clamping bolts. The cylinder head has masked spark plug holes (¼″ dia), with $2^3/_8$" hemispheres, as the standard Nine, to meet fuel regulations for the TT event but with pistons which gave a compression ratio of 8.5:1[16]. Racing plugs with recessed contacts bed down on to copper seats in the shrouded plug wells. The cam timings have been increasingly experimented with down the years and the Ulster has not been exempt. However the original timing set for its TT form used a different inlet cam which gives an opening of 18° btdc and a closure of 50° abdc, a timing geared to long duration road racing where immediate returns were offset against low stressing. The dwell on this cam is set at 248° and the exhaust cam at 254°. This gives an overlap of 42° with tappets set at 5 thou where the 'standard' Imp timing produces an overlap of 62°. A letter from Rupert Riley to the proprietor of Grosvenor Garages in respect of the engine fitted to AVR 718 states an ignition timing on the Ulster of 25° btdc while the maximum available on any combination, as quoted earlier according to J.A.Robson[17] is 36°. The Ulster's camshafts are of the vintage pattern – used in conjunction with a BTH magneto and the end float is taken up by a disc forming part of the camshaft which locates the cam against the rear face of the large camshaft front bush. To the front of this is a camshaft thrust race. The gears themselves are non dished steel, machined and lightened[18]. Standard vintage cam gears and the later dished type gears are both cast iron.

---

[16] see page 26 regarding TT fuel regulations and their effects.

[17] op cit p 42.

[18] See photos pp 68 & 69

Driven off the side of the inlet cam gear a smaller skew gear at right angles drives the magneto mounted above while below it, Brooklands style, sits the water pump, but is unique to the Ulster range of cars. This differs from the Brooklands pump in that the up-thrust on the shaft of the gear drive, is taken by the bronze bearing and its housing. The impeller is smaller than that in the Brooklands, as is its housing and the whole more efficient. The magneto is driven by a dog mounted to its shaft on a taper with a woodruff key which seats in a housing on top of the water pump shaft, allowing easy removal of the Magneto without disturbing timing settings. The drive shaft was mounted in a wax and corded seal above the water way, pinched in a bronze seating bolted down onto housing studs, but a modern sealed bearing has often replaced this. The impeller and water way on this pump is much smaller and more powerful than the Brooklands equivalent. Waterways are appropriately fed by hose linked copper piping, offset into the radiator tanks. An Aric temperature gauge probe is mounted in the thermostat housing forming part of a double elbow into the header tank.

The twin 30mm SU carburetters mounted on the Brooklands box-style two stud manifold are pressure fed by a dash mounted hand pump from the large fuel tank with a threaded filler cap. Drive was transmitted to the 19" wheels through a centrifugal clutch and through an ENV type 75 preselector gearbox with deep sump as was fitted to the Q and R and the last 10 K3 type MGs[19]. This is heavily finned and with additional drain points to the standard Type 75 box fitted in the standard Imp. Ratios originally fitted for the TT are (1st) 3.4:1, (2nd) 2:1, (3rd) 1.36:1 and (4th) direct, with a 5:1 back axle ratio. Reverse ratio is 5.07:1. Over the years on some cars ratios have been changed and other gearboxes fitted. The propeller shaft is supported in the torque tube by a roller bearing held in place by a single retaining bolt visible on the top of the torque tube, and the rear axle nose piece is of electron. Half shafts are waisted for lightness as are steering linkages and many other parts. The rear axle is retained in place by U bolts over caps made of electron, resting on shallow electron spacers raising the under slung frame by 2¼" against the standard car. Semi-elliptic rear springs have nine leaves and fronts have seven as on the standard car. However, all have forged rather than rolled eyes. Hartford shock absorbers are used front and rear. The braking system is common to both types of Imp though the Ulster has roller bearings in place of plain bushes in all its brake cable pulleys, and integral strengthening webs on the front back-plates. Camshafts are larger diameter and the rear brake camshafts use hollow tube rather than solid.

Steering is by worm and segment set in a full wheel electron steering box, and lever controls mounted on an aluminium column with its 17" steering wheel, give timing and hand throttle adjustment, as used on the prototype Imp and on the Brooklands model. An oil reservoir with a direct feed to the sump was fitted under the nearside scuttle with filler cap visible above this and a charging pump fitted beneath the n/s dashboard. Instrumentation provided a large rev counter to 6000rpm, ammeter, temperature, oil pressure and air pressure gauges, fuel being pressure-fed by hand pump. A Rotax panel provides magneto on-off, lighting and starter controls, again

---

[19] Information provided by Mike Allison (P/S Gearbox and MG specialist and author)

The body of AVR 718 during restoration in 1985. Layers of paint being stripped to discover the original dark blue colour scheme with its racing roundels

as fitted to the Brooklands. Twin 6-volt batteries are mounted behind the seat squab and a shallow shelf provides space for the spare wheel to be carried over the fuel tank. A rudimentary hood was provided, with a small tubular "umbrella" stand on the rear body with loops on the front screen mounts to tie it in place!

Bodily the two types of Imp greatly differ. The Ulster racing body was a single alloy skinned tub with slim steamed ash framing reinforced by a good many mitred metal plates, overall considerably lighter than the standard car in consequence[20]. The boat tail does not transfer to the road Imp due to a differing body line[21]. It was held in position by two bolts passing either side of the fuel tank up into captive nuts in the frame of the tail. For ease of access, over centre externally mounted clips have appeared in place of this arrangement. For the TT, to comply with regulations a fold flat windscreen was fitted, using fittings of the type used earlier by the Gamecock but with gauze rather than glass, while the occupants actually used the protection of aero screens mounted on the rear of the larger screen.[22] An under-tray was fitted running from the front bulkhead to the rear of the tail in two sections. The bonnet has an offset hinge allowing generous access to the engine from the offside and is retained in situ by two leather straps with locating loops. The bonnet top panels' louvres are of two differing types. These Ulster bodies were fitted on both the Racing Nines and on the Racing Six. They occur later as on the Densham special, taken perhaps from ADU 300 or ADU 301 (qv). The Dobbs 12/4 used one. He had one of these bodies fitted in 1934, by the Works to (thought to be) an MPH frame with 1500cc engine though he replaced this shortly afterwards in favour of the lighter offset single seater.

---

[20] see lower photo p 65
[21] see also p 73 (top picture) and p.150 (text)
[22] see photo pages 30 & 38, 124

5 - Imps in Sport

From its introduction the Imp was intended to continue the sporting reputation that Rileys had established over the preceding years. The first sixteen cars produced were all so used. With the exception of the first two cars and 6024981, they come in batches, falling into two engine series (247.. and 411..), both batches including the 7 web Ulster engine, so suggesting that they all did. From the second group, engines absent from the list are numbers 41180, -82, -90 and -94, these also indicating the pattern of components being drawn forward, here in registration date order, viz:

Chassis no	Date	Engine no	Reg No
6024449	7.4.34	40106	KV 8025
6024450	7.4.34	47676	KV8026
6024755	30.4.34	24755	AYK 597
6024757	15.5.34	24757	KV 8932
6024758	15.5.34	24758	KV 8933
6024867	1.6.34	41174	KV 9475
6024868	1.6.34	41176	KV 9476
6024870	11.6.34	not known	KV 8990
6024981	4.7.34	not known	-
6024990	not known	not known	(Australia)
6024992	27.7.34	41178	ADU 162
6025034,	18.8.34	41192	ADU 300
6025035	18.8.34	41196	ADU 301
6025038	18.8.34	41188	ADU 302
6025036	22.8.34	41184	ADU 303
6025037	25.8.34	41186	AVR 718

There is one batch of three frame numbers, others in pairs, engine groups overlapping, showing their release pattern into the competition department where they were built. Dates of registration as shown also illustrate this. There are one or two here with no known history at all, but the rest are known to have been built to competition specification.

Setting aside the show car, (which may have worn KV 8026 for a time[23]) which has some reasons to claim identity with chassis no 6026133, and which was fitted, like the rest of this group, with a competition engine, the first Imp to appear in 1934 form in the general production run was chassis no 6024449, KV 8025, a car which continued in rallies and promotional work, for some time. This included the opening of the TT course in Sept 1934.

Their debut was in the 1934 RSAC Scottish Rally for which four cars were entered. For this, the cars wore standard coach-work but had competition mechanics with

---

[23] See footnote, page 7 and on Riley's use of registrations see the caption to Works photo on page 181 upper photo.

The Racing Six prepared for Dixon and Paul, KV 9478, for Le Mans (Riley Record)

preselector gearboxes. They assembled on Friday 18th May at Hadfield aerodrome. AYK597 was driven by Miss Dorothy Champney, (later to wed Victor Riley), Eddie Maclure drove KV5392, T.C.Griffiths had charge of KV8025, C.A.Richardson drove KV8933, while A.J.Dickson joined the company in the MPH KV5694. (See photo page 2). While Miss Champney made her own way to Edinburgh, (with the Le Mans trip to follow hot on the heels of the Scottish Trial), the other four cars travelled by way of the MCC London - Edinburgh trial. For them the route travelled overnight to Harrogate. After breakfast, the trial hill of Park Rash was cleaned, and a stop and restart at West Stonesdale. Then on to Brough, Penrith, Keswick and the Honister Pass. After a lunch stop in Carlisle, came Talla Linn then to the finish in Edinburgh where the five cars were reunited. On the Monday, they embarked on the event they had come for. On the first day Maclure's car put up second best time in class 1 as did the Richardson MPH in class 2. Driving tests on the promenade at Aberdeen was Tuesday's main activity with a reception and a tea dance, once that was done. More driving tests followed on Wednesday while Thursday involved a 300 mile return run from Strathpeffer with some tests included in the earlier part of the day thence to Glasgow and the finish. Twenty three teams in all finished the rally and in the results announced on Friday May 25th Rileys had done well in Class 1 with 1st, 4th, 6th, 7th and 10th places and Miss Champney with a hat trick had again taken the Ladies prize, Rileys also winning the Light Car class for the third time. The Riley Motor Club No 1 team (Griffiths, Maclure and Richardson), had taken the outright team prize and the No 2 team of Champney, Maltby (in another MPH) and Dickson were third. TC Griffiths in KV8025 was the outright winner of the Light Car Class.

Following this, the Champney Imp, AYK 597, returned to Coventry for some preparatory work for Le Mans. The car was fitted with cycle wings for this event and a four branch exhaust requiring bonnet modifications as photographs indicate. In fact while the Scottish Rally had been running, the two companion cars destined for Le Mans had been completed and were road registered. These are described as "specially prepared Imps with slightly modified bodies" - the word Ulster is not used, though the formula for the racing Ulster Imp was here laid down. These followed the design and modifications described already (see pp 15f). Alongside them were two (12/6) MPHs built up on the Grebe chassis that had run in the 1933

22

Beside the maroon Champney / Petre Imp, the Ulster Imp KV9475 , as No 39 for Trevoux & Carriére in the Le Mans pits due to finish 12ᵗʰ   © Photo by kind permission of Coventry Transport Museum.

TT. These used the same body format as the racing Imps including the detachable tail and the beautiful lines of these racing MPH cars is seen on page 22. Of these, KV9478 was no 28 for Freddie Dixon and Cyril Paul, destined to come 3rd, and KV 9477 was for Sébilleau and Delaroche, (race number 27), which came second overall. Von De Becke and K.S.Peacock were meanwhile to drive the Brooklands KV 5392, (race no.36), which, following the previous year's success, won the biennial cup, and was 5th on distance and 1st in the 1100cc class and 1st on index of performance. Of the two 'special' Imps, KV 9476, (Race no 37), finishing 6ᵗʰ, was driven by Sammy Newsome and Edgar Maclure while KV9475, (Race no 39), was for Jean Trévoux & René Carriére. This car came 12ᵗʰ. The cars were fitted with Salora headlamps along with side & tail provision.

One French commentary on the event praised Riley's successes with some force. It noted that Von de Becke's Brooklands came home fifth behind the winning Alfa, two Riley MPH's, and a blown 1100 MG K3 Magnette, while the first Imp was only 3 Kilometres behind Becke on total distance. In fact Rileys had taken 2ⁿᵈ, 3ʳᵈ, 5ᵗʰ, 12ᵗʰ and 13ᵗʰ places without mishap, beaten outright only by a supercharged Alfa Romeo of 2.3 litres! Behind these were two 1½ litre Singers for the Hon Brian Lewis and Stanley Barnes, coming in 7ᵗʰ and 8ᵗʰ places, a lone Type 44 Bugatti followed and two LM 1½ litre Aston Martins. The next unblown 1100 cc car home was an Amilcar in 14ᵗʰ place. In all a very worthy effort by Rileys.

The Imp of Mrs Kay Petre and Miss Dorothy Champney, was running in standard coachwork as race number 38, and drew attention in practice as well as in the event. Night time driving was part of the practice requirement and to this end the course was closed to other than competitors between 10pm and 6am. The Riley Record recounts, *"One would see the neat figure of Mrs Petre springing into Miss Champney's Imp at midnight. For a couple of hours the little red car would drone steadily round the course. Then it would disappear. At 4am it was back again with*

23

Dorothy Champney came 13th and won the Ladies award at the fastest time for a woman driver of that time (photo Riley Record)

Miss Champney at the wheel and the faithful "Meester Charley" Griffith sitting yawning on the pit counter. In the event itself, Trevoux had a bad skid at Mulsanne dropping him down to last (44th) place at the end of the first hour, a mechanic having to do some work on the car's boat tail. The heat was telling and the ladies' car needed attention in the almost tropical afternoon allowing Miss Champney to change her shoes(!)." [24]

According to son Victor, matters were more complex than that. Victor (Snr) was late arriving and the race began in his absence. Dorothy, somewhat distressed mismanaged her start by catching her finger in the Imp's door and proceeded to bleed profusely, dressed as she was in white overalls. She drove for an hour trying but failing to staunch the blood and dropping back finally into last place. She went into the pits, had her hand bound, changed overalls and shoes all of which had suffered, received a sprig of heather for luck from Victor, who by then had arrived, and set off again in a cleaned up motor – still lying last. Thus recharged she made up ground quite quickly until, when lying 13th, the pits signalled her to slow for the car's sake, and this position she and Kay Petre obediently retained to the end, bearing in mind that KV9475 was only just 25Km ahead. She was somewhat frustrated by this direction, as she thought that the car was capable of more and could have come higher. She and Victor married not long after!

The Trevoux car in the following hours also climbed its way back up through the field. By 7pm Dixon was lying 7th. At 3a.m. Von de Becke had 91 laps to his credit and was lying 3rd with Dixon scoring 90 laps and in 6th place. A crowd cheered in the late stage of the race as Dorothy Champney hastily refuelled and at the finish the

---

[24] Riley Record account, October 1934

Remnants of her Le Mans run – the Bonnet strap loops- on the Champney Imp, AYK 597 in Belfast for the Ulster Rally prior to the TT. ©Belfast Newsletter by kind permission.

ladies scored the highest speed achieved by women drivers on the Sarthe circuit.

While Le Mans was absorbing interest, there was action at home for others. The promotional work in trials went ahead and was well publicised. Harold Goodwin entered the Riley 100 (North West Centre) Trial, driving KV8025. Also in June Victor Riley driving one of the new Imps put up some good times and gained a second class award. Returning from Le Mans (June 16th and 17th), Dorothy Champney took her Imp on the1934 Women's Automobile and Sports Association, (W.A.S.A) High Peaks Trial held that year on 14th July not long followed by the Ulster Rally at the end of August.

This Rally was the call up for the Tourist Trophy, the 7th on the Ards circuit. Of the 42 entries Riley's mounted no less than ten cars, eight Imp '9's and two racing MPHs of 1458cc. Cars were required to complete 35 laps of the twisty 13 mile circuit. Rileys entry was as follows. Cars no 30 and no 31 were Le Mans racing sixes, the remainder were Racing Ulster Imps:

Race no	Entrant	Driver	Reserve	Reg no
30	Dixon	Dixon	Brackenbury	KV9478
31	V.Riley	Staniland	Sébilleau	KV 9477
32	V.Riley	Von der Becke	Sébilleau	KV 9475
33	V.Riley	S.H.Newsome[25]	Sébilleau	ADU 301
34	V.Riley	E. Maclure	Sébilleau	ADU 300
35	Dixon	Cyril Paul	Brackenbury	KV9476
36	Dixon	Pat Fairfield	Brackenbury	ADU 302
37	F.E.Clifford	F.E.Clifford	-	ADU303
38	W.R.Baird	W.R.Baird	-	ADU 162
39	A.Freeman	H.B.Prestwich	C.W.Provis	AVR 718

---

[25] Newsome can be identified in ADU 301 wearing grey overalls as Race no 33, while Becke in KV9475 drove in whites with a cloth helmet while the others wore whites & crash helmets.

The TT pit area stretched out along the roadside. In the foreground KV 8025 acting as course car, beyond it one of the ex Le Mans 'Sixes', then No 34 with no lights. Bill Greenaway (mechanic) with cigarette (Photo from a private collection)

The formula for this event had been toughened progressively. The trend towards thinly disguised racing cars was being resisted and standard production models were intended. Newly, superchargers were banned and while lamps were not required, wings and hoods were obligatory this time and a screen (usually a wire gauze) was fitted in fold flat state and fly or aero-screens used. There were also minimum dimensions and cars of engine capacity exceeding 1500cc must carry four seats. "Freak" compressions were ruled out, (The Light Car Aug 31.1934), as fuel mix was limited to a maximum of 50% benzole. "Catalogue" cars were required which perhaps explains why the brochures for the Ulster and standard Imp were represented by KV 8025 on the brochure for both models.

ADU 300 for Maclure receiving final attention. Note the 'umbrella' hood mount,
Including Eddie Maher on right, then Edgar Maclure, Sammy Newsome in helmet, Bill
Greenaway.(nicknamed 'The Baron'), Percy Maclure, (Photo from a private collection).

The chassis' were standard production frames apart from the minor featured differences (see p16-17), and other manufacturers also used lighter more streamlined bodies.

For this event, unluckily Dixon was not able to compete following an earlier accident at Donington Park. As the entrant for two "Nines", he was very critical of the ratios the cars were having to use which conformed to those generally fitted in what was intended to be a good all round sports car. Expectations were high as to how Rileys would fare, none the less, and Riley's reputation built up in successive successes lives on in the Province even today. However the Riley Record notes that the Riley engineers had

"grave fears as to the advisability of running the only cars available, namely the Imp models. These cars were capable of almost unlimited thrashing and suitable for high speeds under all the conditions of every day use, rather than maximum performance on a particular course."

27

Near the start: from left to right: Paul, Becke, Maclure, Newsome, Baird, Prestwich, Clifford, Fairfield. Curiously Paul's ex Le Mans car has no stone guard. (By kind permission © the Goddard Collection)

As a result, we are told, the engineers carried out an experiment on Newsome's car. While the gear ratios were fixed, it was permitted to vary tyre size and oversize tyres were fitted to his car. On this factor his position of 16th – one of the last to finish – was blamed. There were other moments to mar Riley's entry. Prestwich had a monumental crash emulating that of Dixon and Gillow, losing the line at Quarry Corner, clipped the verge, ending in a ditch with the car on top of him. The ditch saved his life but he provided historians with a detailed record of under tray, gearbox type and much more![26] Bobby Baird, who carried a riding mechanic, caught fire and stopped to extinguish it, briefly continued on but had to retire. Clifford completed only 30 laps. On the plus side Von der Becke recovered for Riley the fastest lap at a speed of 71.48mph after Hodges had taken it to 71.37 in his 1100 Singer. This did not, however, measure up to Dixon's lap in 1933 of 77.69. In the final results, Becke came 9th and was first in class G for the 1100cc cars, with a handicap factor of 2 laps. Maclure came 11th, Fairfield 12th and Newsome 16th, respectively taking the 4 class places. That said, the two Singers had trouble, Klemantaski's entry failing to start and Hodge going out with steering failure. The MG Magna of Ashton Rigby did not qualify, leaving Rileys to fight it out among themselves! In Class F, for the 1100 to 1500cc cars, which were credited one lap, Brackenbury failed to start while Staniland went out with engine trouble after 21 laps. The following two years, Jack Chambers raced his Brooklands each time but in 1936 he ended both his race and the series with his disastrous crash at the Newtownards railway bridge with fatalities and injuries. In that fatal year Bobby Baird once again ran his Ulster Imp but went out after 17 laps with engine trouble.

---

[26] Eg see p 39 lower photo

Becke in distinctive helmet leads the works cars, Newsome (grey overalls) trails. (© LAT Photo)

After the 1934 event, one car, which may have been a spare for the TT but not used, was shipped to Australia to the Riley distributor Bertie Cohen. This was driven into 1st place by Bill Williamson at the Nov 24 1934 Maroubra 2-litre Championship. The car failed to finish in the Jan 1st 1935 Australian Grand Prix but in the Benella '100' created a new record for unsupercharged cars lapping at 79 mph with an average speed for the event of 76.1mph. Rileys benefited from the ensuing publicity. A nicely detailed photo overleaf of Williamson at the wheel authenticates this. The car came second in the Benella "100" race near Melbourne in 1936 with two other Imps finishing 5th and 8th. George Thane drove his Imp in the 1938 Australian GP but retired with a broken crank. Whitehead's ERA won. In 1947 B.Myers came 12th driving an Imp in that year's Australian GP.

Another export after the TT was Clifford's car. This was advertised and found its way to South Africa bought by Buller Meyer, seen on p.31. He had a number of successes with this car, including a second in the third South African Grand Prix in 1937 behind Fairfield in the 1100cc ERA. Of the other Imps that raced in the TT, details such as are to hand are spelled out in the individual profiles that follow. The two Le Mans cars survived but ADU 300 and ADU 301 were not to enjoy such destiny and were broken up on 16th April 1935, and the log books surrendered, as the Works sales records state, then in the hands of Arnold Farrar. ADU 301 was to reappear later as will emerge. AVR 718 was raced pre-war but then had 37 years in retirement till returning to active use as is recounted below. Undoubtedly, ADU 302 probably has had the most extended racing career passing through the hands of a number of exponents of the sport and along the way gaining a silent third gear box and hydraulic brakes. T.C. "Cuth" Harrison had it from A.F.Ashby in 1936 and came 9th in the 1938 TT and so that it could qualify it gained a pair of doors! He fitted the Silent 3rd gearbox finding the ENV ratios too wide for circuit work and consistently suffering top gear slip. Post war it was raced by A.D. Underwood and later by Phyl Sutton in VSCC events. It is still very active today in the hands of its present owners.

Williamson at the wheel of Ulster Imp chassis no 6024990. Note distinctive body features. The car came second in the Benella "100" race near Melbourne in 1936. (© Private collection)

"B. Bira", like Mike Hawthorn and Mike Spence, started his racing career in an Imp. Well written up, in Prince Chula's accounts of his young nephew's racing career, is the story of the purchase of BLL170, its development by Thompson and Taylor's at Brooklands and his early successes prior to graduating to an MG Magnette. After T&T's treatment the car gained a top speed of 87mph. According to Bill Boddy, [27] (in an oblique comment on the handling of the Imp), at his first race at Donington in May 1935, Bira "made up on the corners what he lacked in speed on the straights". While he moved on to the so well known exploits with his ERA, the Imp continued in use especially as additional transport, and even as a practice car for learning road courses at Dieppe, and elsewhere. This Imp was also used in some trials, as a diversion from the main development of his racing career. C.A.N. May colourfully describes Bira arriving to take part in a 1935 MGCC "Rushmere" event, but asking where on a Sunday morning he could buy some competition tyres more suited to trialling…[28] There is no trace of this car today, following research, and believed broken up according to Nerisa Chakrabongse.

Another lost Imp is CME 412, owned and raced and rallied by A.L.Phillips. This appears in a picture in the Riley Record at Starkey Corner at Donington at a 1935 J.C.C. meeting, the car coming third in one race and first in a five lap handicap. Philips tellingly recalls the Imp being *"wonderful to handle, firm on corners, and very responsive. The self-changing gearbox enabled one to keep both hands on the wheel when most needed".*

---

[27] The Motor Sport Book of Donington, p.40

[28] CAN May,*Wheelspin.* p 47.

ADU 303 after its arrival in South Africa in the livery as Clifford had raced it in the TT (photo supplied by Rodney Green)

AD Underwood in ADU 302, 1952 May Silverstone – the Maidstone and Mid Kent race meeting (a Ted Walker Photo ©)

Phyl Sutton in ADU 302, at a VSCC race meeting in the 1960s

Baroness Kohler might be driving BGP 530 or BGW 119
(Riley Record Photo).

Here an Imp ALJ 454 competes in the Lawrence Cup trial. (© The National Motor Museum)

Imps were subjected to a good deal of rally and trials use in the following years. Baroness Kohler competed in the Hungarian Reliability Trial in 1935: 250 miles from Budapest to Lillefured and back, "beating cars of considerably greater capacity" according to the Riley Record.   A Miss M.Anderson in an unknown car in both 1935 and 1936 competed in the Monte Carlo Rally as did another Imp, BYV466 driven by Moncrieff in 1936 starting from Stavanger in appalling weather to his undoing. This also ran in the Bo'ness speed hill climbs.   In 1935 a team entered the RAC Rally,   John Archer in WS 2374 gaining a first class award, J.Porritt in ATT392 a 2nd and C.V.Wells in a black Imp, BPL1, gaining a 3rd. Wells won a 1st class award with a clean sheet in the same car in the 1935 Exeter Trial. (See also p 176 & 201). He went on to become secretary of the North West London Motor Club. Likewise in the RSAC Rally, Archer again used WS 2374, Charles Sleigh used WG 3688 and Miss Freda Walker drove VH7503.   Archer again got a 1st in the 1936 RAC with WS 2374. Mrs Freda Elliott (married by this time), in VH 7503 again entered the 1936 RSAC rally, Midge Wilby was in the 1935 and '36 Welsh rally and Philips in CME 412 in the 1936 Blackpool rally.   These and other details are to be found in Donald Cowbourne's work, *British Rally Drivers and their Cars*.[29] Another name that features in pre war rallies and trials is Miss K. Lysley but here another car identity is so far untraced, though the lady driving in the Lawrence cup above might be she in ALJ454!

Further afield, in 1936 two Imps and a Kestrel 9 won the team prize in a tough Australian Light Car Club's 24 hour trial climbing at times to 4000 feet in the Alpine Range near Victoria on hazardous roads in pouring rain. The Riley team, (M.Wreford, C.Keefer & W.Wallace), two Imps and a Kestrel did not drop a point!

One exponent of trialling post war was Cyril Bold, (later RAC Trials Champion in his Ford Special), who made very effective use of the Imp WS 2374. C.A.N.May describes the scene at the first SUNBAC club meeting on 10th September of 1945

---

[29] 'British Rally Drivers and their Cars' Published by Smith Settle

Cyril Bold, Trialist in Action also in WS 2374. (Source not found)

at which "Cyril Bold put up best performance of the afternoon on the aggregate of placings in the four events put together." Bold's name accompanied by his 1089cc (sic) Riley appears frequently in the pages of the book that recounts the post war return of serious trialling. At the Mar 6th meeting, 1946, starting from the Royal Oak at Gretton, Glos., May describes one test where "Bold's Riley did a 'wall of death' turn on the offside bank to such an extent that Cyril confessed to me afterwards he thought the car was going over."

In the fifties and sixties some Imps were modified for greater performance by fitting the 12/4 unit. This seems to have been most common in Australia, one case fitting a 6 cylinder as will be seen in the profiles that follow. One European example is the Imp belonging then to Willy Oosten, who competed extensively , fitting an engine swapped from a Kestrel Sprite. The Kestrel Sprite was afterwards described as a Sheep in Wolf's clothing. In one event he made special use of the flexible engine and traffic clutch this recipe gave to the Imp. He was up against Aston Martins and Porsches. On one test with a gate opening routine, the drill was to stop in front of the gate, open it remove a ball from the left hand post, drive through the gate, close it and replace the ball on the right hand post; some task for a solo driver, involving much furious braking, sprinting, stopping and accelerating. But Oosten jumped out of his Imp approaching the gate, he sprinted ahead of his car, tore open the gate and removed the ball. The Imp obediently trundled through on its own. Willy closed the gate, replaced the ball, ran after the car, leaped in and disappeared in a cloud of dust to the amazed on lookers. In the Alpine rally of 1950 or 51 he was well on with a clean sheet when overreaching in a speed test, he blew a piston. Out of the rally, he fitted a new piston from his on-board spares and continued on into Italy where he finished second in class in the following Evian-Mont Blanc Rally.

On the following page, this atmospheric study comes from the Bill Becke collection of Walter Gibbs. (now in Guy Griffiths collection). It dates from Dec 1951, the car in the hands of E.J.Laker, who had recently acquired it. Possibly a VSCC Trial at Wisley. JM 4370 is alive and well today.

Oosten at Zandvoort

In more recent years, Imps continued to be well used, though it has to be said that their appearance in trials is virtually unknown, in part due to low ground clearance, (4″ at its lowest point), though treating them tenderly is more likely to be the cause. They appear at rallies, driving tests and speed events but the drift from being working cars to becoming a preserved species, partly to be blamed on rising values, is taking its toll and as values continue to climb this trend intensifies. But there are those who continue to campaign them as was intended in hill climbs, rallies, driving tests and some other speed events.

Testing times.......

Prestwich makes final preparations on AVR 718 for the TT – Baird's car is alongside. (Photo © by Hugh Cocker)

Hugh Cocker was a friend and racing partner of Bryce Prestwich and was there in the crowd for the 1934 TT at Quarry Corner and saw Prestwich crash. Together they had raced a number of cars including the GN Tiger III which Cocker had bought from him. After the TT Prestwich did not race the Ulster again, but raced an MG Magnette including a win at the Cork International in 1937 ahead of a 2.3 Alfa. After the Ards TT, the Riley was taken back to Burnage Lane, Levenshulme where Grosvenor Garages (the entrants) repaired it and repainted it red. Cocker bought the car by a whisker, just beating a telegrammed bid from Frontier Garage, East London, South Africa, trading in his own Imp (chassis 6025340 "Black with green upholstery"). Cocker used the car in a number of events and in the next four years raced regularly. Circuits included Donington, Southport, and Phoenix Park, Dublin. He fitted special Martlett Pistons and raised the Compression Ratio to 12:1 running on 60% Pratts Ethyl Special and 20% Benzole and 20% ordinary Ethyl. This would just pull 6,200 rpm giving 103 mph. Rupert Riley had warned him not to take the revs above 5,500 and dismantling the clutch revealed one centrifugal weight about to break away. Thus the clutch was removed and a hardened shaft made up after shearing in a race at Donington, broached by Rileys for direct drive to the gear box. For racing at Southport, the steering ratio was raised by fitting a longer drop arm, again with the help of Rileys. He came 6th in the Southport 100 mile race in 1936. In 1937 in the search for more speed he fitted a lighter, lower body, and set the original aside into store to be re-fitted later.

37

Prestwich ready to go in the 1934 Ards TT. Is the red mist rising. Note details of screen and other original features. (printed with kind permission © the Goddard collection)

The 1934 TT, here Baird, Newsome – already dropping back, and Prestwich, coming down towards Newtownards off Bradshaws Brae. (© the Geoffrey Goddard Collection)

Prestwich has overtaken Maclure running into Quarry Corner and heads into disaster on lap 6 ,where Dixon and Gillow had gone in previous years as below – both © Goddard Collection pictures

Prestwich to the far left. The ditch saved the driver's life. Note the under tray and special ENV gearbox .

Racing at Southport in 1936. The 100 Mile Car Race © Cocker

Southport again, Race preparation, now wearing the lighter temporary bodywork © Cocker

Donington Coronation Trophy meeting, 12.5.37. - Clifford Nash, (31),Goodacre (27) P.Maclure (36) Cocker (35) (Photo – the Light Car)

Wetherby Sprint 1938 - Cocker in AVR 718, running here with the lighter temporary bodywork

Like Prestwich, for Cocker, Club racing at Donington was the main interest including a win in an 'All Comers' Six Lap handicap in 1938 and a win in a Fraser Nash event in which he delighted himself by beating the Nashes at their own meeting. In 1939 Cocker was called up and also got married. He put the car back

Honeymoon preparations in 1939 - the car with some minor mods, re-united with its original body

together again but discarded the temporary lightweight body. For Phyl, his wife's, added comfort and extra luggage room, he moved the spare wheel out on to the off side having already mounted the air pressure fuel pump on that side of the scuttle where he found it easier to reach. By this time the car was black and the bright work had been painted over. Front wing mounts were slightly different and the car was still on the 7.00 x16" rears that are to be seen in the later competition photos. Cocker joined the Army and sold the car to an airman friend, John Hibbert who had access to aircraft fuels on the understanding that he would buy it back "after Christmas when the war was over". During the war, Hibbert taxed the car for one year only, and while on active service in North Africa married an Egyptian girl. He sold the Ulster in 1945 and it remained in Cumbria, bought by Bill Robinson who had considerable successes as a works' driver for Jowett in rally and circuit, winning the 1½ litre class in the 1951 Monte Carlo Rally in a Jupiter. AVR718 then went to Bill Slinger. James Ormerod of Accrington bought the car in 1947 and used it very little. He had last taxed the car in 1956. The author bought it in 1984. Curiously enough, each sale of the car was transacted by 'Jack' Freeman's company Grosvenor Garages, apart from this last. It is believed they had sold out to Henley's some time earlier. After the war Cocker joined ERA and worked for them for many years. A note and photo from the author in *Motor Sport* in December '84 searching for previous owners brought a phone call from Cocker re-uniting him with his old car. Visits and exchanges ensued. Cocker, a lifelong member of the BRDC died in 1992. Prestwich, having followed his father into the cotton trader shipping business in Altrincham ran a Bentley before and after the war. Tragically he was killed, together with his wife, Joan, and their two daughters in 1956/7 in an air crash at Greenfield near Oldham. A son survived them but was later killed in a train accident.

AVR718 as acquired by the author in 1984

Hugh and Phyl Cocker reunited with the car in 1985 at the start of restoration work

43

Cornering through Comber during the TT anniversary celebrations 1986 organised by the Ulster Vintage Car Club - the author and his daughter. (© Esler Crawford Photo by kind permission)

7 – Practicalities

As a touring car, the problems of luggage space in Imps have been variously addressed over the years. The small well behind the seat squab provides for hood storage on a folding frame with something left over for small items[30]. The adage is around that the car was designed for the young man who had access to more than one property where his other suits were kept and only a tooth brush was needed to bridge the gap in essential supplies! The Company actually made a small valise at a cost of £5 in material which matched the interior car's trim to fit the space[31]. Two examples are extant. Various bulkier attempts have been made to provide luggage racks but fail to avoid top hamper as the following page and page 93 show!

Sometimes there is variation in the diameter of the dished housing for the spare wheel. While original equipment fitted was 4.50 x 19" tyres, some new brands of tyre will only sit proud of this housing. Modern 4.50x19 generally present a problem.

On the matter of lighting and electrics in general, the output from the Rotax 3-brush constant charge dynamo has given owners down the years cause for concern. But normal standards of maintenance and care coupled with the occasional rewind should set such worries aside. And today there is the added benefit of halogen and LED bulbs which can fit directly into the existing housings and can greatly reduce the requirement of valuable amps.

---

[30] See illustrations pp 146 & 148
[31] See pp 85 and 161

Photos by Alan Lomas, showing 6025512 with luggage rack mounted, date – sometime in the 1950s

Michael Hetman & Company from Berlin touring in Imp BXV671 near Montlhery, 1999

45

8 - Memories and Moneys

In 1954 Dennis White was hunting an Imp and looked at ADU801 at a dealership in either the Croydon or Beckenham area at an asking price £225. He drove the car noting its scruffy condition and Silent third Box as fitted by Mr C.E.Piggott who remarked when he bought the car in 1937, 2 years old - that it had not been well treated. In the 60s, the offer of NKD 494 was a private response to his advert for an Imp, priced at £375. CMV 91 was similarly offered, and at a price of £325. The author bought his for £220, in 1962, but soon they started selling for more than their original 'new' price. BRA763 was for sale with Chequered Flag for £395 and BUW 904 was offered at £375 by Performance Cars of Chiswick. George Birrell bought CMV 91 for £295 but sold it on when he found the then immaculate BYY909 for £425. The displeasure of Tony Bird, then editor of the Riley Register Bulletin rose when one Imp passed the £500 mark. Still small beer by today's standards! Three cars have recently changed hands for well in excess of £60,000. Rileys in general are tending to sell at higher prices than has been customary, they perform well, are reliable and durable and parts availability is good. But the upward trend in prices always risks the growing interests of the collector and their disappearance from both the eventing and the ordinary motoring scene.

Another Scottish Rally memory, Dorothy Champney's Imp enjoys a picnic as much as more serious action! Jessie Agnew sits on the running board according to Victor Riley. (A Riley Record Photo)

46

9 - Listing of Riley Imps

Chassis Number   6024449

T.C.Griffiths takes the Lochinver test in the 1934 Scottish Rally (Riley Record)

Original Registration No   KV 8025
Date of Registration   7 March 1934
Original Engine Number   40106
Gearbox type   ENV Wilson preselector

History. The first Imp in general production. A Works Demonstrator and much used in publicity for the new model. As with the other cars used in the Scottish Rally this car would have had competition mechanics. See notes on 6024755. In the picture overleaf, note the early type screw-on filler cap. Driven by T.C.Griffiths in the MCC Edinburgh trial and in the Scottish Rally of 1934, the car won the Light Car Class. Appeared in subsequent sporting events in the hands of Harold Goodwin among others. Dismantled by Works pre-war, according to Arnold Farrar.   Last owner according to Coventry registration records was the Riley Motor Company, Durbar Ave, Coventry. Photos of KV 8025 appear on the publicity material for both the Imp and the Ulster Imp.

The famous brochure shot of KV 8025 as used on both the Imp and Ulster Imp publicity. Note the fuel filler – initial provision for intended twin spares? But see also pp52 & 53 with standard fillers. Apparently, the girls in the office were used to additions to their work of this sort. Some say it was because they fitted the car better than some of the men! (Riley Record)

E.J. .Wilkinson opening and closing the roads at the Ulster Automobile Club's Hill Climb at Craigantlet in 1934. 'Northern Whig' photo © with thanks.

Chassis Number 6024450

© LAT Photographic

Original Registration No KV 8026
Date of Registration   7th March 1934
Original Engine No   47676

History An entry in the 1934 RAC rally. Thereafter shown dismantled on Coventry City records. A case could be made for this to be the '33 Show car: clearly visible are raised scuttles, Lynx style screen, differing wing form etc. See footnote on page 7 and pp.116ff.

Chassis Number 6024755

Photograph taken circa 1985 at the Coventry Riley Register Rally

Original Registration No AYK 597
Date of Registration   30 April 1934
Original & current Engine No 24755

Gearbox type	Wilson ENV Type 75 preselector HR
Body style and type	Standard Imp sports body
Body Colour	Maroon, later black, now green
Wheels & Tyres	Wire centre lock 19" Maroon now green
Trim	Standard Road car trim, maroon

History 1934 team entry in Edinburgh trial, and the Scottish Rally, followed by the Le Mans 24 hour race, finishing 13[th.] Race no 38. Driven in each event by Dorothy Champney and Mrs Kay Petre. Victor Riley sold this car to the Managing Director of Bristol Aeroplane Co for his son's use, who subsequently is supposed to have written it off. An apprentice to Fairy Aircraft acquired the parts but failed to complete. Stanley Burville next owned it and rebuilt it. It passed through various hands including (from 1947): D.P.Jones, Barry Austen, A.W.Oxford, John Puttick, David Pitt, and again Stanley Burville who in 1960 sold it to Mrs V.D.Fraser who parted with it in the late 1980s, thence to John Young. Coys had it for sale in 2001 and it has been to Japan and back via Holland, since.

This and the following two cars, have matching chassis and engine numbers, unlike other Imps. Along with KV 8025 these four were all used in the Scottish Rally. In a 'Blue Diamond' overhaul in 1976 Ian Gladstone noted a competition engine with triple plunger oil pump, BTH magneto and water pump to Ulster specification, also a racing crank with additional balance weights and hollow big end bolts, sub sump on an Ulster sump, forged spring eyes, and the tie bar slimmed between track rod ends. The car also had retained its early bonnet with loops for bonnet straps – marks of its Le Mans history. Regrettably these have been removed. Stone guards are a standard fitting on Imp radiators. But here (see previous page), the mounting differs, reason unknown.

The Engine bay of AYK597 photographed in the 1980s, showing the BTH Magneto mounting above the Ulster type water pump. An SU electric pump provides fuel supply on the standard bodied cars. Round rocker boxes were introduced with the Imp and the external oil supply to the rocker boxes is visible as is the drive to the rev counter. The 1$\frac{1}{8}$ " carburetters are mated to a Brooklands type manifold.

Chassis Number 6024757

Photo: M.McQuire

Original Registration no	KV8932
Date of Registration	15 May 1934
Original Engine no	24757
Gearbox type	Close Ratio Silent Third (originally ENV)
Rear Axle ratio	4.89:1
Body style and type	Imp sports body but shortened wings fitted in 1938. Red with black trim
Wheels and Tyres	Wire centrelock, 3" rims, 18 x 500 front and 18 x 5.50 rear. Colour silver

History One of three Imps entered for the 1934 Scottish Rally in which it was driven by Eddie Maclure. Retained by the Works, appearing in an Imp advertisement in the June 1934 issue of The Riley Record. According to Pau Scholes it was bought for H.W. (Bill) Startin (Percy Riley's Nephew and possibly his godson), on passing his matriculation in 1938. The chassis, axles and cable brakes were from a spare car for the 1934 Ulster TT and these remained in the racing department, dismantled, until Rileys gave up racing in 1937. Startin acquired the car, thanks to family connections, and it was built up with a standard Imp body, special series engine and ENV Gearbox. Startin later acquired brakes from Percy Maclure's 2 litre with MPH drums and special Girling back plates and made up a crash box with parts gained from Bob Gerard. He replaced the full wings with cycle type wings from a K3 Magnette and was building up a special racing engine when war broke out. It is possible that a chassis change took place in this process or even later as there is a case to be argued that this group of cars were fitted with the chassis having front spring pins on the centreline of the front cross member and with forged spring eyes. (see page 17). In the mid '50s Startin parted with the car because of family commitments and it was subsequently owned by Lt Pagden then P/O F.J.Smith. It passed into the hands of Stanley Burville in 1959, who fitted a set of full wings. The racing engine had been destroyed during the bombing of the factory, so a standard modified unit is now in use. This uses the large crankshaft, 9½:1 compression ratio, and a camshaft overlap of 60 degrees. A masked (vertical) plug head is fitted with enlarged valve ports. Cooling is now by fan assisted thermo-siphon. Abbreviated wings have now been refitted, together with large Hartford shock absorbers, by the present owner. See also p156 on 6027667.

Exhaust side of engine on 6024757. Thermo siphon cooling and special exhaust

Chassis Number 6024758

Works publicity photograph in Riley Record. Note twin spares mounted (The Riley Record)

Original Registration	KV 8933
Date of registration	15 May 1934
Original Engine number	24758

History   The specification for this car would match others in this trio with matching engine numbers. Driven by C.A.Richardson in the 1934 MCC London-Edinburgh trial and the Scottish Rally. Subsequently sold to Mr & Mrs N.Train of Hamilton. The car was destroyed by fire in 1939, tragically being declared a total wreck.   A dismantled engine remained from this car but its condition and subsequent history are unknown.

KV 8933 (with AYK 8025 & KV 8933), its team mates, for the Scottish Rally, driven by Colin Richardson in the foreground. Note wheel colours differ. (Riley Record photo)

"Here's one we prepared earlier", a publicity shot of KV 8933 in the making . (Works photo)

Chassis Number 6024867

Photograph taken at Gaydon 1998 Riley rally.

Original Registration	KV 9475
Date of Registration	1 June 1934
Original Engine no	41174, still fitted.
Gearbox type	Wilson ENV
Body Style and Type	Ulster Imp racing body,
Body Colour	Dark blue with red trim
Wheels and Tyres	19", Wire centre lock. Silver. Also 15"16"17"

History. This was one of the two "specially prepared" Imps[32] for the 1934 Le Mans 24 Hour race: entrant no 39, driven by Jean Trévoux and René Carriére to finish 12th overall, and 3rd in class. It lost two laps in the pits for repairs to its tail following "a bad skid at Mulsanne"[33] Consequently, it was running 44th, and last, but finished 12th overall and 3rd in class. With race no 32, in the 1934 TT at Ards, it was driven by Bill Von de Becke who won the class and was 9th overall[34]. The Works sold it to John Gee who raced it at Donington Park, Southport etc. After World War II it went to Bloomers of Grimsby and in July 1947 to Walton on Thames where John Heath and George Abecassis built HWM racing cars. Fred Hobbs worked at HWM and drove it at the Brighton Speed Trials. In 1947 George Lighton bought it from HWM, and two years later returned it. Leslie Hawthorn owned The Tourist Trophy garages (T-T) at Farnham. He knew the staff at HWM and had met Lighton and he bought the car for his son Mike for his 21st birthday.

---

[32] see page 22ff
[33] Riley Record July 1934
[34] see pp 25ff

Leslie also bought an Imp from Francis Beart who had built it up. "The best parts"[35] were selected for Mike's car. The T-T Garages converted the 13" drum cable brakes to hydraulics. Four Amals were fitted using Freddie Dixon's method of tuning each cylinder individually. Mike drove the car in this form to take seven firsts, three seconds and a third in eleven outings. In August 1952 it went to John Riseley-Prichard who raced it with the Cornhill Racing Team. In Feb 1953 the car was fitted with a 1496cc Riley Sprite engine. The radiator was moved forward to accommodate the larger unit, the small chassis cross member having to be bowed accordingly. The original 1087cc engine was refitted before the car was sold to Ian Jordan for £235 via Lexham Garden Motors. He sold it again in about 1954 to a dealer (as it turned out) in Rochdale. In 1957 it was advertised in *Motor Sport* and Mike bought it back He embarked on a rebuild, but died in a road accident on 22 Janaury 1959. After this Tim Ely purchased the partly dismantled Imp from Mike's mother for £150. Over the next four years he rebuilt it. Following Mike's preference for a centrally mounted gear lever Tim made a zig-zag shift mounted on an alloy tube from the Wilson gearbox. He also fitted a smaller alloy fuel tank accessed by the tail being hinged, a dummy filler retaining the original "look". Packing below the rear axle gives a lower line to the set of the car. Hydraulic brakes were retained but Lockheed backplates were used with12" Alfin Drums, obtained from Fred Hobbs at HWM. In 2003 a Ronco Scintilla Vertex magneto was fitted sitting on a reduction gearbox. The car has telescopic shock absorbers. Tim has many original parts which could facilitate returning the car to "standard".

The engine bay as at present showing radiator in its forward position, carburation provision, and special magneto and cooling arrangements. Note the reversed head. [36]

---

[35] quoted in Hawthorn's biography p 20 Challenge me the race"
[36] see on this chassis No 6027668

The car still wears Hawthorn's bow tie as its insignia and under the raised apron are anti-tramp bars to tame the front axle. Note the Hydraulic shock absorbers but also the Ulster aligning of the front springs to front cross member. The upper cross member has been bowed to allow the more forward position of the radiator

Interior arrangements with the modified gear selection and instrumentation

Chassis Number 6024868

Photograph taken circa 1980 of earlier owner George Taylor with the car

Original Registration No	KV 9476
Date of Registration	1 June 1934
Original Engine No	41176
Gearbox Type	ENV P/S deep sump, no 4233. 13.5.34
Body style and type	Imp Sports with cycle wings and spare cover
Body Colours	Blue with black trim
Wheels and Tyres	5.00x19" fronts, 5.50x 18" rears

History. The other "specially bodied" and much modified Imp along with 6024867 was prepared for the 1934 Le Mans 24-hour race. It was driven by Sammy Newsome and Edgar Maclure No 37, which came 6th overall and 2nd in Class. Cyril Paul drove it in the Ards TT in September 1934 as race no. 35 but only completed 21 laps. In 1935 George Taylor the next owner heard through a friend of Cyril Paul that a team car might be available. Rupert Riley met George and introduced him to the Competition Department workers. George chose the standard Imp body to use it as a road car, needing hood and side screens.   He then took him for a drive stressing that the reconditioned engine must be run in. Many miles later George took the car back to the Works for a de-coke. David Venables recalls his first sports car ride in this as a 4 year old, his father being a rowing friend of George, the families holidaying on the Suffolk border. At this point the car was stolen and recovered but with a broken gearbox, the clutch bob weights having burst the bell housing[37]. David recalls bits of gearing on the roadway. The car was overhauled by the Winter Garden Garages where Taylor part exchanged the Imp for the Works Aston Martin LM21. He stated on a tape recording that the Imp would reach 85 mph quite easily and was very impressed with its road holding and reliability. The present owner acquired the car in 1969 from an elderly couple who moved to Cornwall in '67 and owned the car since 1938. They discovered its unsuitability for taking dog and the washing on a weekly 20 mile round trip.

---

[37] See p.37

57

According to Frank Hawke, the car retains all the bodywork and extra instrumentation, also the original competition engine as supplied to George Taylor. The crack tested racing crank with detachable balance weights, hollow big end bolts, racing con rods and 3/8th small ends. The engine, with a 14 pint sump was completely rebuilt and upgraded in the early 1970s. All internals were polished to mirror finish and balanced and the camshafts were re-profiled to racing specification. New 9:1 pistons were lightened and balanced. The triple eccentric oil pump was fully re-conditioned. The original body was rebuilt, as was the chassis and fitted with cycle wings, small petrol tank and aero screen over 4 years. A single span bonnet with louvres was fitted in place of the standard Imp bonnet. The front axle and steering arms were nickel plated, springs polished and early steering gear and Mk IV levers retained. The car won the Maher Muller trophy at Riley Register Coventry Concours 1975, where it was displayed in the hotel foyer. 1974-1978 it was raced at VSCC Events, in Circuits and Hill Climbs.

A 'working' shot - Silverstone Paddock in the 1970s. Note the MPH style tail and body with doors.

Chassis Number 6024870
Original Registration Number KV 9550
Date of Registration   11 June 1934

History: nothing known about this car other than Coventry registration details. Thanks to research by Peter Banner in city records.

Chassis Number 6024981
Original Registration No   None known
Date of Registration   4 July 1934

History: Coventry registration details. Also researched by Peter Banner in city records

Chassis Number 6024990

Photograph in Riley Record - Wilkinson in Melbourne Centenary Nov 1934

Original Registration no   Not confirmed. EJ 176(Vic) from 1945
Date of Registration   not known
Now fitted with a 12/4 engine

History   This car was a spare for the 1934 TT race but was neither used nor raced in the UK but was sent to Australia to be raced by the Australian Riley distributors, main agent Bertie Cohen, with Bill Williamson as driver. The car had several successes in late 1934 including fastest lap at 79 mph and an average speed of 76.1 setting a new record for an unsupercharged car at the Maroubra Speedway in NSW. At Philip Island on the Jan 1st 1935 he drove in the '300 Centenary' race, and on 1st April 1935 in the Australian Grand Prix but failed to finish due to gearbox failure. Various other events followed including a 2nd place in the 'Benalla 100' in 1936. At this stage the car is said to be equipped with an Ulster engine, on a Compression Ratio of 11.8:1.

Details of the original body conforming to the TT set up are illustrated on page 30. During the 1940s that body was discarded and replaced with a lighter body saving 190 lb leaving the fuel tank sides exposed. Around 1940 Ron Head had brought Sprite racing engine components from the UK and built up and experimented with a supercharged 1500 cc 12/4 unit for the car and replaced an ENV gearbox with a close ratio Brooklands box. On 26 January 1948 in the 13th Australian GP, at Point Cook, Victoria, the car then described as an IMP Special, came 10th driven by Ron Head.

Alex Mildren of Sydney bought the car and continued to race it including the 14th April 1952 Australian G.P at Bathurst NSW. Due to Magneto problems at the start he lost 6 laps but with skill and courage he passed 36 out of 43 cars only to be black flagged for receiving outside assistance. After this John Marston brought the car back to Victoria but appears not to have raced it till 1958 at Geelong Sprints. Ross Chillianis then bought the car and raced it at Fishermans Bend and at Albert Park where the engine failed due to a broken con rod.   Plans were started to fit a 2 ½ litre Riley Engine and Holden Rear Axle but the project did not go ahead.   From 1965 on, the car passed through several owners without more work until Lance Dixon had Ern Langford build a new body – a cross between an Ulster Imp and a Sprite, and Ian Ruffley did some chassis repairs.

Ian Ruffley bought the car in 1983 and is using this body but is now fitting a blown 12/4 engine and Brooklands gearbox for hill climbs and sprints.

The car, probably at Hurstbridge hill climb, Melbourne in 1947, when owned by the Head brothers. Note raised scuttles on the new body but also the Ulster chassis front spring mounts. (RMCA photo)

Chassis Number 6024992

Baird in Comber Square in the '34 TT , unlike the other entrants, with riding mechanic. Body not narrowed at this stage. (© Blackstaff Press photograph)

Original Registration No	ADU 162
Date of Registration	27 July 1934
Original Engine No	41178 Later fitted No 25620
Gearbox Type	originally ENV, now Silent third C/R
Body style and type	Racing Ulster body, lowered and narrowed
Body Colour	Mid blue, with black trim
Wheel size	Various, mainly 16" painted silver

History Full spec Ulster Imp but with specially narrowed racing body, carried out during Baird's ownership. Subsequent special features including an inclined plug head but with direct coolant line to header tank and double plunger oil pump on the replacement engine.

Prepared for Bobby Baird for the Ulster TT at Ards, race no 38, sold to him via Leslie Porter of Belfast. Baird was not happy with the car which caught fire on lap 6 at Dundonald. Baird raced again at Phoenix Park in 1934 but retired after 3 laps. And again in the 1936 TT. Around 1939-40, the car was sold to Vic Leverett, Riley's sales manager who saw it advertised. The body had been narrowed and modified lowering it by 2", by the time the car was sold. This is shown in pictures from Leverett's time and in wartime trim, this work done by Rileys. History is unclear from then on, Henry Geary acquired the car in 1962 and had developed and raced it extensively with great verve. It then passed to his daughter on his death, who with her husband has completed a rebuild and is continuing its use in competition.

A photo at the Riley Works circa 1940, the car in war time road trim, with Vic Leverett at the wheel but showing the modified bodywork : narrower than the chassis and with the altered line at elbow level

61

The modified cockpit and silent third gearbox of ADU162

*The Ulster Imp magneto and water pump system in ADU 162 but with cable advance and retard.
(photo taken circa 1990)*

Chassis Number 6025034

No 34 at Quarry Corner during the '34 TT. (© LAT Photographic)

Original Registration No	ADU 300
Date of Registration	18 August 1934
Original Engine No	41192
Gearbox type	ENV pre-selector
Rear Axle ratio	5:1
Body style and type	Ulster Imp racing body with detachable tail
Body Colour	Blue
Certified dismantled	16th April 1935 in Works register

History. Full spec Ulster Imp with racing body. The gearbox would have been of the finned deep sump type with special ratios.

Prepared for the Ards TT race for Edgar Maclure, a works entry for Victor Riley. Race no 34, the car completed the required 35 laps and came 11th overall and second in class. Jean Sebilleau as reserve driver. The car was broken up by the works in the Spring of 1935 and the registration book surrendered, as entered in the Works sales log.

Chassis Number 6025035

Rodney Green at the wheel of the re-created car in the 1990s

Original Registration No	ADU 301
Date of first registration	18 August 1934
Original Engine no	41196
Gearbox type	ENV
Body style and type	Recreated Ulster racing with detachable tail
Body colour	Dark Blue with black trim to Ulster style
Wheels and Tyres	19" Centre lock, colour cream

History This car was prepared as race no 33 to be driven by Newsome as a member of the team of three Ulster Imps entered by Victor Riley in the 1934 Ards TT. Driven into 16th place, and 4th in class, running on oversized rears in an attempt to address the suitability of the gearing of these cars for the circuit. Jean Sebilleau was reserve driver. After the race the car was dismantled and the registration book surrendered on 16th April 1935 as noted in the Works Sales Register. As was the pattern, according to Arnold Farrar, parts, including the chassis might be sold on as used spares, in this case to J.C.Bamford also acquiring a Sprite engine and gearbox. (See the notes on chassis no 6025085 in this connection). Sold on to Ken Gillibrand, as GRF 899, the car went to South Africa in 1959, owned variously by, Mike Gluckman & Jolyon Simpson. It was acquired in 1983 by Rodney Green who researched on the history. The chassis number 6025035 was later found on the front dumb iron and verified by the Vintage and Veteran Club of South Africa, the later number 6025085 being the first number found but stamped on the frame alongside the steering box mount. The 12/4 engine and other gearbox had been accommodated by moving the mid placed cross member of the frame back by 70mm. In Green's ownership the housing for the 5.25 rear axle from a saloon was machined to conform to Ulster shape, and a new engine was prepared to Ulster spec by Neville Farquhar, with Allen crank and rods, Ulster Imp Sump, Ulster type water pump, all mated to a type 75 ENV gearbox with new bell housing and gearbox sub sump from a Rapier and CG gears in place of HR gears. A reproduction radiator shell was produced and a new core made up. Hightone Restorations built a new body, copied with permission, from Chassis no 6025037 with continuation work and fitting by Jarvis who has gone on to make other copies. The complete car has competed in S.African & British motoring events and included completing the 1991 Mille Miglia. The car has passed to new owners in the last few years. (See also 6027477)

This photo taken at the time of discovery of the remains of the car in the 1980s shows the chassis stamping but also the form of dumb iron on these competition cars where the spring eye (forged) locates on the line of the cross member. On the standard Imp this mounting is raised by 1".

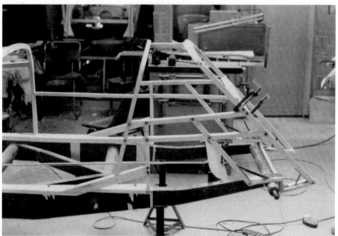

Re-creation of body frame for ADU 301 by Hightone Restorations, Oxon in 1985, showing the lightweight ash frame structure used in these bodies.

65

The re-created ADU 301, Silverstone circa 1988

Von der Becke in KV 9475 leads the works cars early in the 1934 TT. Newsome, in ADU301 car no 33, distinguished by his grey coloured overalls, and with oversized rears. In other photographs Becke, in white overalls and linen helmet is shown driving car no 32. (Photo © LAT Photographic, and the Riley Record, Oct 1934).

Chassis Number 6025036

The restored condition of ADU 303 – photo John Harmsworth

Original Registration no	ADU 303 currently ND 637 (South Africa)
Date of registration	22 August 1934
Original Engine No	41184
Gearbox type	ENV P/s, deep finned sump type No 2424
	Dated and stamped 17.4.34 C31
Rear Axle Ratio	5:1 with Electron nose piece
Body style and type	recreated Ulster Racing with detachable tail
Body Colour	Mid Blue, Originally Green and Cream
Wheels and tyres	19" Centre lock
Trim details	Black

History . Full spec Ulster Imp with 7 Web block, triple plunger pump, Ulster sump, now with Allen crank, Corrello con rods with shell bearings and high compression pistons, rear springs have forged eyes, recreated racing body. The pictures overleaf detail some features of the Ulster Imp engine.

This car was prepared for F.E.Clifford, a private entrant in the 1934 Ards TT. It was flagged off after completing 30 laps. On January 8th 1935. Clifford advertised it for sale in <u>Motor</u> for £395, colour cream and olive green. (see page 29 and upper photo p 31). Thames Garages, with help from Lord Howe sold the car to Buller Meyer in South Africa, who raced it in the 1937 SA Grand Prix on January 1st. coming in 2nd place at an average speed of 77.09mph. It came 3rd in the 1938 SAGP at 74.93 mph driven by D. Richardson. The Ulster body was discarded and a smaller lighter sharply pointed tailed body fitted, believed to be the body from TT Sprite CWK171. This was further modified and the car put to a variety of uses, some agricultural till the engine blew.

John Harmsworth who had worked on it in the '50s re-acquired the car in the 1980s and constructed a new body, mainly copied from ADU 302 and carried out a very thorough restoration. The car still very active, remains in S.Africa.

The car as acquired by John Harmsworth with Sprite style body

Steel cam gears, as fitted to the Ulster Imp, and the timing chest, on next page, showing the recess for eccentrics for the triple plunger pump as fitted to the Ulster Imp (All photos on these pages, courtesy of John Harmsworth)

68

The triple plungers are driven from the rear of the idler gear as in the case of the double plunger system on the standard Nine engine

The deep sump ENV Box as fitted to the Ulster Imp with modified selector linkage in the case of ADU303

69

Chassis Number 6025037

Photo by John Warburton at Shelsley Walsh Hill Climb 2007

Original Registration no	AVR 718
Date of registration	25 August 1934
Original Engine No	41186
Gearbox type	ENV finned deep sum type, No 4237
	Dated and stamped 17.4.34, C11.
Rear Axle Ratio	5:1, Electron nose piece
Body style and type	Ulster Racing body with detachable tail
Body Colour	Dark blue with white roundels to original pattern, Dark red upholstery recreation of originals which remain with the car. Black tonneau. Pre war specimens retained
Wheels and tyres	19" Centrelock in black with 4.50x19 tyres

History Prepared for Grosvenor Garages of Manchester entered in the Ards TT by A. Freeman, driven by Bryce Prestwich, reserve driver C.Provis. Race no 39, the car crashed at Quarry Corner. The car was repaired by Grosvenor Garages who advertised it. Hugh Cocker, a close friend and racing colleague of Prestwich purchased the car and raced it subsequently at Donington, Phoenix Park (where the car was clocked at 95.7 mph), Southport etc., from 1936 – 1939. The car was re-bodied with a lighter TT Sprite shaped body, and the original set aside, but at the outbreak of war and Cocker's marriage, the original body was refitted. Cocker sold the car and subsequent ownerships are detailed on page 42. The author, John Gathercole bought it in 1984. The car was complete except for a missing ARIC temperature gauge, and was generally very untidy. Repainting revealed white roundels under layers of red, black and blue paint. The dark blue today matches the original dark blue found under the roundels. The car has been used in competition since 1986 at Donington, Silverstone, Cadwell Park and Oulton Park and at Prescott, Shelsley Walsh, Wiscombe, Loton Park, Croft and Craigantlet Hill Climbs. It has also been back to the Ards TT reunions in 1986, 1993 and 2003 and has won several Concours including the Riley Register's Maher-Muller Trophy and is featured in Mark Gillies book ' the Golden Age of the Riley Motor Car'.

The car is full spec'n Ulster Imp with original racing body, racing crank, hollow big end bolts, 7-web block, K805 rockers, lightened cam followers, masked plug head, triple plunger oil pump, forged spring eyes and a CR 11:1, Omega racing pistons now replacing very smokey Martletts! The rear of the block has a strengthening plate as were fitted to many Nines by Horace Richards, though this one was fitted by Hugh Cocker himself. Nines have a reputation for weak casting at this point. In 2006, the ENV Box was rebuilt by Mike Allison and ratios changed to 3.1, 1.84, 1.31, 1. Recent successive visits to a rolling road, after needle and other adjustments, produced 77bhp at 5,100 rpm at the wheels and a steady torque figure from 2,500rpm of 75 ft/lb, showing the capability of these 1100cc engines.

AVR 718 alongside KV9475 at the start of the Ards TT Commemorative run 2003 Note AVR's offset bonnet hinge. (photo by Duncan Cartwright).

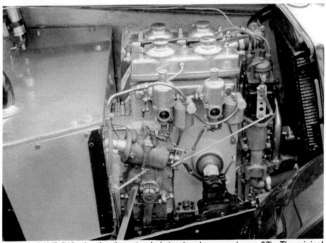

Engine of AVR 718, showing the extended steering drop arm. (see p.37). The original hessian cover over the bulkhead boxing has been replaced by aluminium.

71

Chassis Number 6025038

Original Registration No	ADU 302
Date of registration	18 August 1934
Original Engine No	41188
Gearbox type	Silent Third fitted replacing ENV
Rear Axle ratio	5:1
Body style and type	Original Ulster racing body with detachable tail with doors fitted for the 1938 TT
Body Colour	Cream with blue chassis and dark blue trim
Wheels and Tyres	19" front, rear used 16", 18" and 19"

History This, the "most raced" Ulster of all was entered in the 1934 Ards TT driven by Pat Fairfield and entered by Dixon as number 36. Fairfield finished 12th overall and was 3rd in class completing 35 laps. In 1935 the car was sold by Rileys to Reg Grice of Grimsby, perhaps via distributors D&AH Bloomer, then to George Briggs in London whose wife raced it several times in '35 & '36. At this stage A.F.Ashby worked on the car, entering it as No 12 in an event on 22 Apr 1935 at Brooklands. T.C. 'Cuth' Harrison purchased it from Ashby in 1936 and raced it in 1937 in several Donington events including the 12 hour sports car race, but it proved unreliable with persistent big end trouble. From its standard form for the '34 TT by the time the car reached Harrison it carried an ali-bronze head with 2 Amals each side and a Laystall Crank, all fitted by Ashby. By 1938 Harrison had reverted to a standard head, 2 standard exhaust camshafts, changed to a Works racing crank, discarding Ashby's parts fitting twin $1\frac{1}{8}$" SUs. The preselector box was changed to a Silent Third with special ratios. In 1938 it was 9th in the Donington T.T. and 3rd in class. For this, doors were required to be fitted to the original body. After the war, it was raced in club events by A.D.Underwood, who bought it from Chiltern Cars, then O.W.Thomas, who converted the cable brakes to a hydraulic system and Borg & Beck clutch. Martin Blinkhorn owned it in 1951/52 Then tuning work was done by Leslie Hawthorn. Stanley Burville had the car and sold it in 1962 to Mrs Phyl Sutton who raced it in VSCC events. She then sold it to Jim Cartwright in 1967 who carried out a major rebuild. It is in successful competitive use today both on circuits and in speed events.

ADU 302 in Ireland for the 2003 reunion of the TT races, organised by the Ulster Vintage Car Club.
After this event, the car went touring on the west coast of Ireland.
Duncan Cartwright took this photo near Clifden in Galloway.

Jim Cartwright at Becketts, Silverstone. April 23, 1988 © Ted Walker

Chassis Number   6025044

Photographed in 1996

Original Registration no	ADU 801, was OSU 163 for a time.
Date of First Registration	22 September 1934
Original Engine No	53938 acc to Works register, now 48406
Gearbox type	Silent Third with extension
Rear Axle ratio	5.25:1 No 53958
Body style and type	Standard Imp sports body
Body Colour	Red with black trim, brown carpets
Wheels and Tyres	4.50 x 19, tyres and Centre lock wheels
Trim	Black, Single pleated seat squab

History This car could be described as the first standard Imp, those preceding all appearing to have competition features and mechanics. In the Works Sales Register, this car set the trend for the cars coming after. It was first produced with a P/S gearbox, and red wheels and an ivory body. It was sold to the dealer Jimmy James on 4th October 1934, who sold it on to Milwards. Other previous owners include Roy Eccles, and C.E. Piggott, (who featured in an   article in Autocar May 21st 1943) . Piggot fitted the Silent Third gearbox, and made up a selector extension, though in those days Brooklands extensions must have been available more than they are today. He fitted bucket seats, side curtains and raised the hood line by which time the car seems from photos to have been repainted in a lighter colour. Piggot comments that having expected the Imp to have a $1^{15}/_{16}$" size crankshaft, he found his had the $1^7/_8$" version. He wrote to Rileys who assured him that his was the correct shaft for the car, but of course, as first general production Imp, it departed from the previous pattern of fitting the racing crank to be found on preceding models. [38]

---

[38] Robson (op cit footnote page 12), gives Crank Pins for the Imp range of $1^{11}/_{16}$", the Merlin of $1^7/_8$" and the Racing Crank as $1^{31}/_{32}$" The Racing Crank has Mains the same as the Merlin of $1^1/_2$" (front) and $1^7/_8$" (rear) while the "Imp" crank has Mains of $1^1/_2$" front and rear. See further pp 12 and 17.

74

Later the car was owned by AGF Dutton in Hertfordshire then by Alexander McInnes (Indianapolis,USA) who claimed fitting a pulley and fan, though as these were standard Imp equipment the need must have arisen, as by this time the engine number had changed. In his time the car wore a 750 Motor Club decal on it's near side. Then on to John Sandlewick, then Chris Hicks of New York followed, who sorted out some electrical problems, supplied horns, correct steering wheel, wiper motor, voltage cut out and oil temperature gauge. At this point the car was yellow with yellow wheels and brown upholstery and carried a spotlight on the o/s screen pillar. The car then had a new owner in Conneticutt before being brought back, first to Denmark and then to the UK. Dan Margulies sold it to John Marr the next owner, the car red with black wheels by now. Marr converted from Magneto to coil and distributor and found it a delight to drive. On re-importing the registration ADU 801 had been lost. Andrew Booth then bought the car. It was again sold to the current owner who lives in Warwickshire and who has managed to recover the original no ADU 801.

One person verifying some of the details of the story is Dennis White, (himself an Imp owner) who saw the car in 1954 in scruffy condition but having the 1932 Silent Third box as fitted by Piggott. Dennis met up with the car again in the UK in 1995 and remarked it still having its crash box.

The non standard gearshift selector for the silent third gearbox, presumed to date back to 1943

Chassis Number 6025048

Peter and Doreen Reece's Imp at Liverpool M.C. Driving Tests, Speke 1953. (Photo Ian Hall)

Original Registration No	GYM 958
Date of Registration	5 August 1934
Original Engine No	Not known, present number 60462
Gearbox type	All Helical four speed, previously an ENV
Body style and type	Standard Sports body with rear spare cover
Body Colour	Maroon with black weather equipment,
Wheels and Tyres	16" to be changed to 19"

History Previous owners include Robert Appleton, Sqdn-Ldr Stephen Blumenthal and Peter and Doreen Reece of the Blakes dealership in Liverpool and who fabricated the spare wheel cover. The car was maroon at this point. The car had been originally painted black when purchased from Blumenthal, when the latter was still in the RAF in 1947. At that time it had twin SU pumps, with bolted up traffic clutch and a Wilson Box which was given to band slippage. An advert in The Autocar in 1949 described the car as having an ENV gearbox, a racing head and 4 Amal carburetters. In 1955 the car passed to Peter Fisher, who fitted a Laystall balanced crank. Tony Birmingham, sometime Riley Register Historian and author owned it next and took it to Naples on holiday, taking in part of the Mille Miglia route. In 1959 it was purchased by Michael Turner, (father of Anthea Turner), who noted in 1972 its undersized wheels, hydraulic shock absorbers, alterations to the front scuttle and batteries mounted in the tool boxes. Other electrical equipment was original Rotax, with a balanced Laystall crank, the block fitted with Cromard liners, and the car reading 60,000 miles. There was no fan at that time nor evidence of one though the car never over heated. It passed through Barrie Gilles workshops around 2000. Recent owners are Peter Ray, and Richard Gray who then sold it to a new owner in 2005. The car now resides in Lincolnshire where it is undergoing a full body, chassis and running gear rebuild, including a colour change to mid-blue with 19" cream wheels.

The cockpit of 6025048 showing the All Helical gearbox in situ.

Chassis Number 6025075

Original Registration no	US8803. Current UK reg'n no RLY 9
Date of Registration	27 November 1934
Original Engine No	54288
Gearbox type	Wilson ENV p/s
Body style and type	Standard Imp sports body
Body Colour	Blue, then white with red interior, now BRG
Wheels and Tyres	19" with 4.50x19" tyres. Colour silver

History   This car was entrant in the Scottish Trial in 1937 as featured in Riley Record.   Later, letters received from the Glasgow Corporation show that using the Registration number US 8803 the car was last licensed and then voided in 1955. At that time the owner was a Mr V.S.White of Newpark Road, Brixton Hill London in '58, R Davies Belmont Surrey, '61. Later owned by Perry Boswell of Frantic Boats, Florida who bought the car from Ronald Davies of Shaldon in Devon. Davies referred to the car as RLY 9 and as having shipped it to it's new owner in 1962.   However, according to Chiltern Cars records, (which may be a date error), it was sold to Mercury Motors of Harrow Road, Wembley who used to advertise their cars in *Motor Sport.*   While Chiltern Cars list it as US 8803, they give a 'registration' date of 27.11.64. But any Re-Registration took place earlier as the number RLY 9 is already connected with the car in 1962, as an article appeared in July 1961 in Road and Track featuring this car as RLY 9, and as in the Register Bulletin (June 1962), the editor, Tony Bird, noting that the £750 that was being asked was "a somewhat inflated estimate of the market value of such a car". Walter Williams mentions in a letter that the number was sold for £25. In 1962 the car wore Lucas biflex headlamps The car returned from USA to the UK and passed through the dealership of C.A.R.Howard in 1987 still registered RLY9. Now in Belgium, the owner having had the engine restored in the 1990s by Barrie Price, the car repainted BRG with black trim now on Belgian plates, featured on a touring run on the previous page.

Chassis Number 6025085*

N. Naylor at wheel at the North Staffs MC Silverstone meeting ,1954 ©Ferret photo

Original Registration No	GRF 899
Date of Registration	1938 See ADU 301, chassis no 6025035
Body style and type	Grebe – like. Nothing more known

History. This car has a short and strange history which is really part of the history of 6025035 qv. That chassis is stamped "6025085" * on the upper face of the frame beside the off side engine mounting and in this form between 1948 and 1959, this car passed through the hands of Stanley Burville and a West End fur dealer before it finally went to South Africa, sold by him to Ken Gillibrand. Burville had bought the car around 1948 from a woman racing driver, who was also a pilot, it is reported. Gillibrand was told that the car had been built up by the Works for a Scottish driver to race in the '35 TT but this did not happen. Arnold Farrar had no note of a reissue of a chassis and firmly believed this would not have been the case. But others say the stores might tell a different story! The car had acquired at some point a TT Sprite engine with 4-bolt con rods with crash gear box, (which required the central cross member to be moved back 70mm), and Girling rod brakes operating large diameter brake drums. Chiltern Cars listed it as the "Baring Riley 1.5 Sports 2 seater, first Registered 29.12.38 and chassis no 6025035" in their sales list some time after 1950. In 1983 it was bought by Rodney Green in South Africa, who on stripping back found the earlier chassis number stamped on the front dumb iron as 6025035 – that of the works Ulster Imp ADU 301[39]. In that ADU 301 was dismantled after the 1934 TT according to the Works register on April 16, 1935, it appears that parts including the frame were reissued as used spares. After a time in South Africa parts of this car went to other users but some were retraced to assist the recreation of the car ADU 301 on this chassis. Green is clear that the later number '...085' is not a misreading of '035'. Here pictured in London around 1959, whilst another shot of the near side shows an exhaust manifold indicating a 12/4 engine.

GRF 899 in London, circa 1959, adds to the mystery, looking deceptively longer than an Imp. A photo of the near side shows the 12/4 exhaust system exposed. (Courtesy R. Green)

---

[39] See the notes on this car page 64

Chassis Number 6025144

Earlier Photograph taken by Peter Sarll

Original Registration no	AVU 808
Date of Registration	20 October 1934
Original Engine No	54350
Gearbox type	ENV Wilson preselector
Body style and type	Standard Imp sports format
Body Colour	White with red trim, black weather equipment
Wheels and Tyres	19" wheels with 4.50x 19" tyres. Colour black
Trim	No sidescreens

History This car competed in a 1935 Winter Trial. It already showed signs of having been worked hard before the 30 years of ownership by Peter Sarll and his wife. They used it to tour the Continent on several occasions. Typically Peter listed a visit to Holland in 1985, the Bordeaux to Bristol "Claret and Classics" in 1987, the Grosser Preis von Berlin in '88, the Lauren Perrier Antibes Rally from Bruxelles to Antibes in 1989, and the Alpes Retro Rally in the Southern French Alpes successively in each year from 1990 to 1994. Peter described the car as then still ripe for restoration but too busy to stop. The car would have done yet more but according to Peter, his wife (tongue in cheek?), disliked the lack of radio, heater, and upholstery, the effect of oil spray on legs and the draught which stopped her smoking to calm her nerves. The car was in Belgium for a short time but the new owner now is in Surrey.

A previous owner of AVU 808 who believed in seeing and being heard – Imps run at 90 °C so keeping cool might be a challenge! (By kind permission © From a collection by A.B.Demaus).

Extracted from a Riley Record December 1935: Harris taking part in the RMC Winter Trial

81

Chassis Number 6025145

Photograph © Neill Bruce

Original Registration No	AOJ 431
Date of Registration	3 November 1934
Original Engine No	54346, but current Merlin engine fitted
Gearbox Type	ENV Wilson p/s
Body style and type	Standard Imp Sports body
Body Colour	Dark red. Fitted twin spare wheels
Wheels and Tyres	19" wheels and 4.50 x 19 tyres, painted silver
Trim details	Black to original pattern

History   A long standing recent owner was Nigel Dawes who sold the car in the late 80s. Prior to this the car had passed through the hands of Stanley Burville, J.V.Thorne '59, & Brian Ash, '61,who fitted a Laystall crank and High Compression Pistons, but as the engine failed to perform sold it on to Tim Ely who found cracks in the bearing housing and installed the Merlin unit, M. Guinchard, Gordon Cussons and Keith Ashcroft succeeded in turn. It appeared much in trade calendars and picture postcards. The car when last seen was fitted with a Merlin engine. The car appears trialling in 1936 in this ©*Ted Walker* photo, reproduced by kind permission.

Chassis Number 6025146

Original Registration No	BGP 530
Date of Registration	14 November 1934
Original Engine No	54340, (a Merlin Engine was fitted for a time)
Gearbox Type	Was ENV Wilson but latterly manual box
Rear Axle details	5.25:1 Rear axle no M24813
Body style and type	Standard Imp Sports with additional screen fittings
Body Colour	Was Black, later Silver grey with black wings
Wheels and Tyres	19" all round, previously 18" fronts and 17" rears. Colour ivory
Trim details	Black with black weather equipment Additional weather screens

History   The log book shows the second owner to be Pat Fairfield[40], Then there is a gap in the history. Keith Chambers completely rebuilt the car but sold it, having an expanding family, asking £350. Tim Ely used the car from 1956 including some competition use and a trip to the Italian Grand Prix. He had continuing contact with Chambers. Other names include HJJ Townsend and RJ Shew. Chiltern cars sold the car to R.J.Law of Brixton in 1963. JK Roberts of Weybridge then had it, fitting a supercharger, which appears never to have been connected but remained with the car. AC Parkinson sold the car on to Dan Margulies and the car was auctioned at Alexandra Palace with some style in 1974 and bought by Reg Ansell. In 1980 the car

---

[40] Autosport 6th Jan 1972 p28

was bought by David Cramer, still with its supercharger mounted and later sold to Gerry Porter. M.G.Mapes then had it from November 1982 but it then passed to the present Portuguese owner. The supercharger, fitted by John Roberts in 1964 was from Tony Crook, but it is unclear if it was used, now removed. Rod brakes were fitted. One later owner disliked the effect the up front weight had on the car's handling. The wings at some point were modified into an unbroken panel, Alfa style, with running ribs passing up the front of the rear wings. A Silent 3rd box replaced the ENV. Twin SUs no longer have air bells as fitted by Tim Ely. The car now has corrected wing shape, dashboard, instruments, hood and side screens and aero screens with their stowage and is back on cable brakes. Additional screen furniture has also been removed. The owner who lives in Portugal also hopes to re-install an ENV gearbox.

Detail of screen equipment as worn by this Imp in the 1980s

Chassis Number 6025217

Photograph of the Maharajah kindly contributed by Sir Anthony Evans.

Original Registration No	SS Wankener 9 1934
UK Registration	NKD 494 Sept 8th 1952
Original Engine No	54482
Gearbox Type	ENV Wilson preselector
Body style and type	Standard Imp Sports body with taller radiator
Body Colour	Maroon with matching maroon trim
Wheels and Tyres	Silver. 500x19" rear and 4.50x19" front
Other details	Original suitcase to fit behind seat with initials

History: This well known, very original Imp complete with Saurashtra Wankaner (India) documents acquired by Frank Hawke 1964. The previous owner had a broken crank replaced by Frank's friend and neighbour, Bert Paynter who was a Riley expert. Frank corresponded with the original owner HH Maharanashree Amarsinhji Maharana Rajsahib of Wankaner, of The Palace, Wankaner. In one of his letters he said that the Imp was his favourite car but it had little use in India. Frank and his wife Elinor used to drive the Imp regularly to the VSCC Beaulieu Concours and Driving test from 1965. The car was a regular Concours winner and in 1971 won the Montague Trophy, best in test and concours. Leaving Cornwall at 5am they also drove to several Riley Register Coventry Rallies to enter the Concours and often returned over night. In 1974 it won the Victor Riley Trophy. With 5:1 CWP, twin 30mm Zeniths it performed well. It has the original headlamps, radiator stone guards but are secured by thin bolts through the core. It was previously sold by Performance Cars in 1954. Ivey- Mollard, of Redruth in Cornwall trialled and rallied the car with some successes from 1954 – 56: see overleaf.

85

W. Ivey-Mollard taking part in the Land's End Trial 1956. © Ferret Photo

Chassis Number 6025218

No Photograph available

Original Registration No	BOL 734 (later re-registered as SNM517)
Date of Registration	11 January 1936 (acc to Bedfordshire County Council and also Chiltern Cars)
Original Engine No	54342
Gearbox Type	ENV Wilson preselector

History.   This car has passed through the hands of Chiltern Cars, sold by them on 18.8.55. to D. Fuller, of Luton. Then to Brian Foyle who sold it to Stanley Burville in 1962. Next owner was PJ McBride of Palmers Green. London, but the last licence was surrendered in 1962. The rear of the car had been modified before Foyle's ownership, according to him, to give more luggage space and with a single door on the passenger side.   The forward part of the car was standard. The engine had been fitted with a Merlin Crank and a single SU and with preselector gearbox which Foyle probably in error referred to as an Armstrong box.

86

Chassis Number   6025259

Photograph taken of N.D.Wakeham touring in 1956, putting the hood up,

Original Registration No	CPA 101
Date of Registration	November 1, 1934
Original Engine No	54344. Now fitted with a Riley 12/4 unit
Gearbox Type	Preselector
Body style and type	Standard Imp sports

History. So far nothing emerges prior to 1955 when the car was sold by Chiltern Cars of Leighton Buzzard to J Parker of Saddleworth Rd, Greetlands, Halifax. Chiltern state that it was fitted with a 1½ litre Sprite engine at that time.   N.D.Wakeham recalled in 1995 that he bought it in 1956 and wrote that the car would knock spots off the MGs at the traffic lights. The car was then red with P/S gearbox, centrifugal clutch and one shot lubrication system which he converted to grease nipples as the capillaries kept getting blocked. The car also then had a 'detachable Brooklands tail', presumably fitted by the previous owner. Later owners include Fuad Mazjub and G.A.Thomas   who had the gearbox repaired.   Another picture in Wakehams ownership appears on the next page.

CPA 101 circa 1957 photo - N.D.Wakeham

Chassis Number 6025339

Action shot of Cyril Bold. - Photograph source not found

Original Registration No	WS 2374
Date of Registration	18 December 1934
Original Engine No	54348
Gearbox Type	All Helical
Body style and type	Standard Imp Sports but variously fitted out for trials use
Wheels and Tyres	19" fronts and 16" rears

History   John M.Archer was probably the first owner who rallied the car (see page 33) having driven it in the 1935 Scottish Rally. Post war it was owned and much trialled by Cyril Bold, who used the car from 1945 and out of sheer affection for it, built a scale model of it in trials form (One wonders where that is today!). Bold was service manager of Braids at Colwyn Bay. In 1946 he took 'Best-performance-of-the-day' award at the Yorkshire Sports Car Club's Wharfdale trial, and gained first class awards in the Jeans, Davis, and Vesey trials. In 1947, first class awards were gained in the Colmore and High Peak trials and he was in the runner up team in the NWLMC event. The car still exists today in Lancashire. It was put back into visually standard form though the dash board, dominated by a large rev counter speaks for its specialised use at Cyril Bold's hands. The All Helical gearbox is still in situ. Whether this is one of the few original A/H boxes for these cars, is not known. Offered as an option (and cheaper), Archer may have chosen this with his competition intentions.

John M.Archer leaving Edinburgh's start control at Stirling, in the 1935 Scottish Rally.
Photo by kind permission of Donald Cowbourne in
"British Rally Drivers and Their Cars", pub Smith Settle

Cyril Bold awaiting the start at the foot of Laverton Hill on the Colmore Trophy trial .
(Autocar photo)

Chassis number 6025340

Older photograph during the ownership of Geoffrey Perfect.

Original Registration No	AXJ 993
Date of Registration	13 December 1934
Other registration	341 MP
Original Engine No	54476
Gearbox Type	ENV Wilson preselector
Body style and type	Standard Imp Sports body
Body Colour	Black. Originally black but post war the car was painted Ivory
Wheels and Tyres	18" centre lock. Now painted red having been silver.
Trim details	originally green trim now red leather with black hood and tonneau

History. First owner of this car was Hugh Cocker who later in 1935 traded the car with Grosvenor Garages in Manchester in order to purchase the Ulster Imp AVR 718. A short piece of home made film taken by Cocker features the car in 1935. Other previous owners include Keith Miller of Southborough (1957-62), Michael Carver '62, Ted Timberlake '63, Coverdale, ('65 –'71) who carried out a major rebuild and had it painted white, Ken Hart then to Tim Dyke, '71-'73, Derek Wedge, Tim Dyke (again!), Peter Agg of Trojan cars during October 1978, Geoffrey Perfect, of Penn, It was auctioned by Coys then Bramley Garages had it for sale at an asking price of £40,000. It features a Scintilla Magneto, bronze bodied twin SU installation. Hart reupholstered the car. Coverdale found that the car cooling system ran at 90 degrees but typically, not exceeded. Fitted with the standard four blade fan. The upholstery was green originally, as confirmed by Cocker. The car chewed up two muff couplings in Coverdale's time and the prop shaft splines were rebuilt with weld. Geoffrey Perfect had major engine work done by Peter Binns, a Brooklands tuning exponent, replacing the exhaust cam and turning it into a "quite rapid little car". It acquired its new registration in Tim Dyke's time. In 2006 the car was sold in Belgium to Sir Michael Kadoorie, and restored to a high standard by Jonathan Wood, remaining in the UK.

Photo taken in the early 1960s by John Coverdale

91

In the late 60s, with undersized wheels. (A.N. Farquhar photo)

Detail of the cable run as originally fitted

Keith Miller makes adjustments prior to the Parade in AXJ 993 at a Coventry –Riley Register – Rally, in the late 1950s. Lionel White looks on. Keith used this car for his honeymoon having driven his bride from the Church in her wedding dress… (A.N. Farquhar photo).

Chassis Number 6025410

Photograph taken by W S Williams circa 1958

Original Registration No	AAD 556
Date of Registration	12 November 1934
Original Engine No	not known, engine no 47250
Gearbox Type	ENV Wilson p/s
Body style and type	Standard Imp sports body - recreated
Body Colour	Now red frame, green body work
Wheels and Tyres	Now green
Trim details	In 2006 being completed

History. Previously well known to Ted Broadhurst who worked for Davis Bros (Motor Supplies) Ltd., in London. A.E. Davis a keen motorcyclist had a severe accident in 1935 and on his final recovery the Company bought the Imp for him from Boon and Porter of Hammersmith, who may have been the first owners and who continued to maintain it. About 1938 it passed to his brother E.S.Davis who kept it through and after the war. Broadhurst drove the car quite often when it was then light grey but it did not have competition use. There is a gap until the car was bought by Walter Williams in Surrey in 1958 as a complete but burned out wreck for £5 from a very distressed seller. Over the years a new body was in preparation. A special engine was part prepared, purchased in the London area. This consisted of parts from AF Ashby from the Flat Iron special, one head with alternating inlet and exhaust flow. Williams had obtained an ex Ashby 7 web (competition) block, Laystall crank with 2" rear main bearing and Glacier rods with Martlett hemispherical pistons with valve

94

cut-aways. Special tappets were fitted with rollers, with separate oil supply, let-in to the foot of each in constant contact with the cams. In order to prevent the tappets rotating, bolts were let into the block running in a vertical groove cut into the tappet. An Ulster sump was fitted. (See p 72 re Ashby parts)

In Dec 2005 Bonhams sold the car to a new owner in the London area as a near completed rebuild. The car now green with red frame on smaller 16" wheels but together with 19" wheels, new loom, lower seat squabs, correct lamps and other parts to finish. The car was fitted by this time with an engine to standard Imp spec, bearing engine no 47250. All the Ashby engine parts were sold separately to another buyer.

The Imp frame of 6025410 during restoration, rear spring hangers, floor panel and running board mountings shown to good effect. A Walter Williams photo.

Chassis Number 6025441

Henrik Schou- Nielsen at a Classics race meeting in Sweden in 2003

Original Registration No	BGW 119
Date of Registration	12 November 1934 (see below)
Danish registration	Was LD 38 489, now K 34 119 (Denmark)
Original Engine No	54472. This was still with the car in the 1990s but a Merlin engine also fitted for a time
Gearbox Type	ENV Wilson preselector
Body style and type	Standard Imp sports largely original
Body Colour	Originally apple green with brown upholstery, now red with tan trim
Wheels and Tyres	19". Silver at the time of the rebuild, now black

History   The date of registration according to Leicester County Council was given as 15 August 1934 but the above date is as given in the log book. It was with T.Davey of Shipley Yorks in 1961 After a long gap, Day of Dagenham sold the car in 1966 to Bob Seymour of Dartmouth, South Devon. A.A.Forbes of Hinckley had the car in regular use in his ownership from 1969, but began a rebuild in that year. He records that the first owner was James Alfred Baxter 31 Spenser St London SW1.

After Andrew Forbes ownership it then passed into the joint ownership of Steve White and Henrik Schou-Nielsen from 1983 - 93 then by the latter, who sold it on in 2003. A single repaint showed that the original colour was apple green with brown upholstery when the car was rubbed down in 2002. The car carries twin spares. The correct engine was still with this car in 1994. Another engine has been fitted, prepared by Steve White, and an ENV close ratio gearbox was prepared by Bill Morris.

In 1986 or '87 Henrik and the Whites toured France in this Imp and in a Lynx clocking up 3,500 trouble free miles from Denmark. The car was recently sold to a new owner in Denmark and is housed in his museum. For a time the Danish Registration was LD 38 489

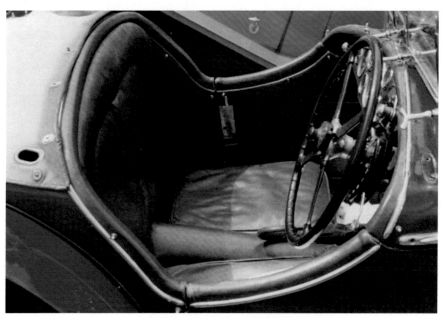

Seating and cockpit layout of 6025441.

Chassis Number 6025442

Photograph taken by John Lee - car when in the Gast motor museum, PA, USA

Original UK Registration No	BLN 196
Date of Registration	17 November 1934
Original Engine No	54360
Gearbox Type	ENV Wilson p/s, Type 75 No 1046
Body style and type	Standard Imp Sports with detailed changes to running boards
Body Colour	Burgundy
Wheels and Tyres	19" with twin spares. Silver colour

History Originally registered in the UK, various owners in the USA notably Gloria Hill and Tom Flannery who regularly show the car in events. Previous owners include Dunstan, and C. Bayard Sheldon of Spring Cove Illinois, who purchased it in 1964, then Charles Williams, and John Moss, all in USA. The running board ribs as on a few other Imps have been taken, (Alfa – style), part way up the rear wings. Brakework patent 320503

Chassis Number 6025443

'59 COOPER FJ T52

'35 RILEY 9 IMP

#6025443 The quintessential British roadster of the '30s, with rare Wilson pre-selector gearbox. Excellent thoughout, continuous chain of owners. Stored for many years, needs some fettling to make it road worthy.

chassis #FJ/25/60. BMC powered in absolutely superb condition, race or show ready; fully sorted out.

'34 AC 16/60 DHC

With pre-selector gearbox; properly stored in dry storage for 40 years, correct, complete and in need of re-commissioning.

BLK 387 re-emerges after a long absence - Motor Sport Advert 2005.

Original Registration No	BLK 387
Date of Registration	November 1934
Original Engine No	54484
Gearbox Type	ENV Wilson preselector
Body style and type	Standard Imp Sports body
Body Colour	Dark red with red trim
Wheels and Tyres	19" Ivory colour

History   According to an American source (RR Bulletin June 2005), this car had four UK owners between 1948 and 1952 and was then shipped to the USA where it had been owned from 1957 by Joe Brown of Colorado Springs. In Dec 1958 it was sold to Blakemore McCarthy, a lawyer also of Colorado Springs who kept it for 47 years with 'minimal' use. It was then offered for sale (as above), by BB One Exports Los Angeles in Motor Sport March 2005, described as the quintessential British roadster of the 1930s. "Excellent throughout, continuous chain of owners, stored for many years needs some fettling to make it roadworthy."

It then came back to the UK for a 'full professional overhaul to be sold at the Paris Retromobile 2006 for £75,000, the highest price paid thus far for an Imp. It was stated that the car has twin Zenith Carburetters and original side screens. Whilst having been re-trimmed the original trim remains and "could be refitted" The headlamps are fully chromed. The car was sold to an Argentinean collector.

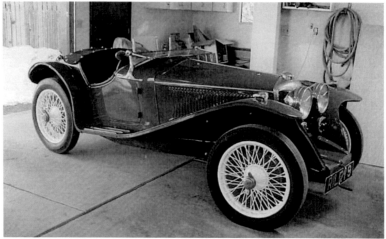

Chassis no 6025443 prior to leaving the USA to return to Europe

Chassis Number 6025444

Photograph unavailable

Original Registration No	AHP 542
Date of Registration	10 December 1934
Original Engine No	54354
Gearbox Type	ENV Wilson preselector
Rear Axle details	5.25:1
Body style and type	Standard Imp Sports, undergoing restoration
Body Colour	Dark Green with 'residual' dark brown trim
Wheels and Tyres	19" with 4.50x 19 tyres. Cream colour Twin spares of 6.00x16
Trim details	Has hood and side screens

History History Registered in Works sales registered to P.Pike and Co Plymouth for Alex B.Craig from November 1934. Other previous owners include Harold Gibbs May 1953, G.H. Bell '59, David Markby of New Malden, Surrey from 1961, Colin Watts of Bridgewater, Somerset, Walter Weiner of Washington USA, Peter Glucklick, Michigan, Chris Hicks in New York from June 1982. The car was re-imported to the UK in the early 1990s and is being rebuilt. The present owner who purchased the car in kit form lives in Kent. The speedometer was missing when taken on by Hicks in what he described as a basket case state. It was wearing a Brooklands type manifold, so lacking hotspot, and has evidence of a previous external exhaust, with a cut away in the bonnet and wing.

100

Chassis Number 6025491

Photograph at Silverstone circa 1996.

Original Registration No	AUB 920
Date of Registration	14 December 1934
Original Engine No	54358
Gearbox Type	Manual – Silent third close ratio now fitted
Rear Axle details	5:1 with electron nose piece
Body style and type	originally Imp sports but now with ' Ulster' style racing with detachable tail, alloy dashboard
Body Colour	Dark blue with black trim
Wheels and Tyres	Silver, 19" with 4.50x19 Tyres

History   Nothing is known prior to 1943,when bought by F.O.Cleveland-Harmer a Rolls and Bentley specialist in Acton who had businesses in Hailsham and Weybridge. He verifies it had a P/s gearbox, and centrifugal clutch. He sold the car, after much persuasion to a "racing motorcyclist" at Brooklands and "friend of Charles Brackenbury who planned to develop and modify it". Thus in 1945 it passed to Francis Beart, who sold it in 1953 having carried out modifications. It then moved on to G.J.M. Birrell, in '53, to George Head, to Joseph Walker of Newbury, (both in '54), then Chiltern Cars. E.T.Eames, a coach builder of Paddington, next "stripped the car completely, removed the old very flared wings and fitted cycle type, fitted mostly new instruments, new type upholstery instead of one bucket seat and then re-fitted most of the new body parts". He returned the car to Chiltern again.

Chiltern Cars advert read, "this potent little car, latterly owned by a world famous engine tuning specialist, is fitted with a 2" counter-balanced crank, latest type of Ulster sump and large oil pump, large port head with 1½" SU carbs and four branch manifold. With a dry weight of 13 cwt it is capable of 90mph with excellent road holding and braking. £295." Phyl Sutton, of Alberbury, Shropshire bought the car in January 1957, at the time when she and husband Jack, owned and were racing ADU 302. It was registered in Phyl's name. Jack noted features which included a Brooklands box with ratios of 13, 9, 6,and 5:1, electron front drums, and a Bowden cable system. Mag was BTH and cooling by thermo-syphon yet he claimed a CR of 12:1. The head had alloy plugs between the plug wells, "presumably to dissipate heat". Road springs have rolled eyes but the fronts are mounted in line with the front chassis cross member suggesting this may be a competition chassis added at some point. The rear axle spring platforms and caps are standard Imp in form.

In 1978 Dick Batho bought it and began to rebuild it with another body. The car was observed at this stage still to have an electron rear axle nose piece (but with standard torque tube), forged spring eyes, and other racing features. Dave Nortcliffe bought the project from Dick's Estate and completed the fine rebuild to a high standard into Ulster Imp form. The car was fitted with a "Nick Jarvis 'Ulster shaped" body from the copy made of AVR 718 by Hightone Restorations for Rodney Green's recreation of ADU 301. Early photos from 1943 show the original car in standard form but having deeply valanced wings as in a few other cases, lacking the formed edge of the majority of Imps, (see page 10), and sporting a radio aerial. The car may now be in Japan. This is, so far, the only Imp with Francis Beart's name explicitly as having been an owner so it is possible there may be connection with the car referred to in the development of Hawthorn's Imp KV 9475 (chassis no 6024867 – qv.).

AUB 920 in Harmer's ownership in 1943. Note the wing valances
(see page 10) and a radio aerial on scuttle.

102

Dave Nortcliffe at Silverstone, in the closing stages of the rebuild of this car. The front dumb irons showing the chassis' competition pedigree are just visible.
(see page 17). The author's wife looks on.

Chassis Number   6025492

Photograph taken by Tony Pearson

Original Registration No	ALJ 454 (and SAA27 1957)
Date of Registration	1 December 1934
Original Engine No	54264 now fitted with 12/4 unit no 35-2956
Gearbox Type	Armstrong Siddeley Preselector

103

Body style and type	Boat tailed body conversion with Brooklands style boot but undergoing restoration
Body Colour	Green
Wheels and Tyres	18" colour Ivory
Trim details	Red trim and seats in leather

History The car competed in the Lawrence Cup Trial (year not known) and also in the Riley Motor Club '24' of 1935. It is featured in Nick Georgano's history of the Sports Car. (Picture page 33 above). The original registration lapsed in 1954 the car then at Long Eaton. Ralph and Maurice Bance of Bordon Hants, bought the car as a rolling chassis from J.Gilman of Long Eaton, Notts. Subsequent owners were Len Luffman, who used it daily also of Bordon, who was considering returning it to original body shape, then to an A.Smith in the Manchester area. The present owner purchased the car in 2000 and lives near Doncaster. Currently the car has Girling brakes, 12/4 engine, headlamps converted to double dipping. The car was built up by Mr Bance using an ash frame with aluminium panelling. By 1957 the car had completed 51,000 miles. To accommodate the new 12/4 unit the gearbox cross member was moved back with a suitable bracket to accommodate the late type handbrake. The torque tube was necessarily shortened. The current owner has a programme of rolling restoration and improvement. "D" lamps have been fitted at the rear and the number plate moved to the side.

12/4 Merlin Engine in situ and re-formed bulkhead today as fitted during the Bance ownership.

Chassis Number   6025493

Photograph taken during Dave Gregory's ownership

Original Registration No	BTW 763
Date of Registration	8 December 1934
Original Engine No	54422
Gearbox Type	ENV Wilson p/s No R 1930HR
Rear Axle details	5.25 IMP No M24810
Body style and type	Restored to a standard Imp sports body
Body Colour	was Maroon, then green, now Sarum blue
Wheels and Tyres	19" Silver
Trim details	Black with black weather equipment

History   In 1960 this car was sold by Chiltern cars to Guy Wyatt. Other previous owners include Alfred Jacobs of London W14 in 1951, Bernard Millington of Petts Wood Kent in 1952, A.H.G.Butler of Wiltshire in 1953, Gordon Brown of Keynsham, Somerset in 1954, Keith Gascoigne of Coleshill Birmingham in 1957, then to Chiltern Cars in 1959 with pointed tail, for sale at £245, Trevor John Dick had the car after Wyatt. Trevor Dick who never drove it having had a nasty accident in a bubble car, sold it to an American serviceman who took it back to USA. It changed hands there and came back to the UK to Dan Margulies from whom Gerry Dick bought it. At this stage it sported a special body with pointed tail and rear cycle wings though the fronts remain firmly Impish. Dave Gregory bought it in 1983 and rebuilt it as shown above and completed the restoration to standard. Wings were provided by Vintage Wings of Stockport. Wynn Williams had the car for a time then it went to Royle cars in Durham. In 1998 it moved to Taunton and now is in west Wales. A new radiator was required and was recently produced by Midshires Radiators of Ludlow.

BTW 763 during Gerry Dick's ownership

Chassis Number 6025503

*In 1975 during Eddie Ashby's ownership. The modified layout retained, following
the fitting of the Six engine, but at this stage with a 12/4 engine. (Photo Noel Wyatt).*

Original Registration   KTV208vic (Australia) (Also 69AGO and IMP034)
Date of Registration   1934 registration Sydney (Australia)

Original Engine No	Not known - 12/4 engine currently fitted
Gearbox Type	ENV Wilson p/s replaced by manual box then an Armstrong Siddeley P/s box
Body style and type	Bonnet extended, now recovered to standard
Body Colour	Was red, then black with red trim, then back to red with black trim.
Wheels and Tyres	18" Ivory

History   Original owner was George Thane, of Sydney in 1934. He entered the car in 1938 for the Bathurst race on the Mt Panorama circuit. Starting 28 minutes ahead of Peter Whitehead's ERA the crank finally broke. A six cylinder Stelvio unit was ordered from the UK with ERA crank and racing rods and a compression ratio of 13:1 used. The bonnet was lengthened and radiator moved forward to accommodate this engine. For a time the car sported 6 1" SU carburetters.   Later the car passed through the hands of Ed du Cros, Eddie Ashby, and Kurt Schulz in Australia. Now carries a longer bonnet, a 12/4 engine, ex Falcon, bored to 1600cc. This was fitted by Ashby with shell bearings, high lift cams, Wilson (Armstrong) p/s box, rear axle from a 2½ litre, twin 1 ½" SU's, and stabilisers for the front Axle. Then in the ownership of Kurt Schulz followed by Pam Zaske a major restoration was undertaken with some work by Noel Wyatt. This retained the 12/4 engine but reinstated the radiator in its normal position. The car was for sale at AUS$205,000 in May 2006 with Ian Cummins of New South Wales .

Chassis Number   6025506

Photo during recent restoration

Original Registration No	JK4309
Date of Registration	at Eastbourne
Original Engine No	Not known Merlin engine fitted
Gearbox Type	ENV Wilson p/s

107

Body style and type   Rebuilt as standard Imp
Body Colour   Red with red trim

History First Registration at Eastbourne. It appears in a photo of the 1939 Southport "24" rally of the Riley Motor Club in the ownership of a Mr J.M.F.Williams. it next appears as a Christmas present purchased as a restoration project by his wife for Leo Juppe of Illinois in 1972. It had been imported into the USA in 1964 into the ownership of a Mr Rollin Weary from whom it was bought. A detailed restoration of the car was embarked on during which a broken crank was discovered. After a some time, it was re-imported into the UK by Gregor Fisken, passed to Barrie Gillies then sold on to Adrian Johnson of Harrogate, who carried out a total restoration as seen on p107 above with a major feature in Classic and Sports Car Dec 1991. The registration number was recovered. In about 1992 the car, in fully restored condition, passed to a new owner in Bingley. At the point of re-importing in 1987 the car had a Merlin block, later type steering column assembly and cover for the spare wheel's spoked area.

Chassis Number   6025507

Photographed by AN Farquhar in the 1960s

Original Registration No   OW 6276
Date of Registration `   8 February 1935
Original Engine No   54368
Gearbox Type   All Helical
Body style and type   Standard Imp Sports body
Body Colour   Ivory with grey (now maroon) upholstery
Wheels and Tyres   18" Colour silver
Trim details   Black hood and side screens

History   Present owners, B.E.Jones, acquired the car in pieces in 1964. Reputed to have a pre-war history of successful competition.   The car may have originally been fitted with a preselector gearbox and the present All Helical gear box may be a later substitution as the gear and brake levers are far too close for comfort and may trap the odd finger if care is not taken.   The engine has a vintage block and the rev counter is driven from the exhaust camshaft.   It has a water pump beneath a BTH magneto perhaps under-scoring a competition history .

Chassis Number 6025510

A happy Arnold Jepson at the wheel

Original Registration No	AUG 865
Date of Registration	1 Feb 1935
Original Engine No	55112, later fitted with engine 54474
Gearbox Type	ENV Wilson p/s Type 75
Body style and type	Standard Imp Sports body
Body Colour	Dark Blue with red upholstery.
Wheels and Tyres	Fronts 19" (4.50x19) and rears 6.00x16
Trim details	Black hood and sidescreens

History Previous owners include Gordon and Glynn, The Riley Centre London SW1, October 1953, HRGHowe,1953, WDByatt,1955, M.G.Maitland, 1956, 1957 to G.B. Buckingham, McGowan Scott, 1960, Michael Nee 1960, Paul Goodley, 1961. Arnold Jepson bought it in 1967 from a garage in Notting Hill Gate, after auction from Paul Goodley. The engine had been overhauled in 1952 for £30. The car's colour was changed to blue in 1958. W.S.Williams wrote in 1972 that Goodley had sold the car to Portobello motors who sold the car on at an increase of 300%. In 1973 the City of Leeds who were the original licensing authority wrote to the effect that the car's registration had been cancelled and the documentation destroyed in 1969, the car having remained untaxed since 1960, the last known owner being Eric Lister c/o Portal Gallery 16A Grafton St London.

In 1990 the engine was stripped and rebuilt having been in poor shape despite a previous overhaul. The body and chassis had been earlier overhauled, the body stripped and repainted to matching previous colour by Ollerton Engineering of Salmesbury, near Preston in 1981. A noisy back axle remained the 'Achilles heel'. The car is fitted with a Scintilla Vertex Magneto and twin SU carburetters. It also has twin SU fuel pumps. On Arnold's sad death in 2007 the car remains in the family.

Chassis Number   6025511

Photograph taken Coventry rally 2001 showing detailing of hydraulic supply lines.

Original Registration No	ATT 392
Date of Registration	January 1 1935
Original Engine No	54424
Gearbox Type	ENV Wilson p/s
Rear Axle details	5.25:1 no 25341
Body style and type	Standard Imp Sports body

Body Colour	Originally grey, then light blue, now black with red frame and red undersides
Wheels and Tyres	19" with 4.50x19 tyres, other sizes in use. Colour silver
Trim details	Re-trimmed red, copied from originals fitted. Black weather equipment

History   The car was advertised in 1951 in a half page advert at £650! The first owner of this car was Joseph Porritt of Torquay who ran it in the 1935 RAC Rally. There is a gap in the war years then came J.C.Payne, then A.A.Rouse, both in Oxford, then Pratt-Barlow and now Peter Banner who, through a long ownership has carried out a major restoration.   During the war years, the car is known to have benefited from an 'essential war work' user, working for Vickers with responsibilities in Yorkshire and Weybridge while living in Wakefield. Pratt –Barlow also used the car between work in Slough while living in Bristol.   Peter Banner, with trips home to Eastbourne had work responsibilities in Stafford and occasional trips to Bradford, Liverpool, Stevenage and Preston. He also used the car for touring and some rallies, all putting it well up among the high mileage Imps.   At some time this car was fitted with a Marshall supercharger mounted on the inlet side and an enlarged o/s bonnet panel allowed for the space required.   Among the cars detritus (sic), are a racing/ Laystall crank, a bent con rod, a broken crank and a shattered bell housing!   The brakes were converted to hydraulic by Horace Richards. The car carried an Ulster large capacity sump, and the traffic clutch is replaced by a solid coupling. See also pp 33 regarding its Trials use, & p161. The car was recently featured in _Classic and Sports Car_ (Feb 2008), linking the sports cars of the 1930s to their use by Airmen in WWII and featured this Imp along with MG K3(s) and Wolseley Hornet. There is ample evidence in this book that Imps were popular among that fraternity.

Chassis no 6025511, ATT 392, in former times with signs of space for the supercharger mounting

111

Chassis Number 6025512

Photo by A.N.Farquhar in the late 1950s: note the pillar lamp, luggage rack and aerial

Original Registration No	BHY 327
Date of Registration	7 October 1935
Original Engine No	54824
Gearbox Type	ENV Wilson p/s No R1625, 13.4.34 R181
Body style and type	Standard Imp sports body
Body Colour	Burgundy red with red, (now beige) hide trim (may in 1958 have been grey with red trim)
Wheels and Tyres	Wire Centrelock, colour aluminium. 4.50x19"
Trim details	Full weather equipment

History Previous owners include Harry Pearson of Leicester in 1950 , Harry Tompkin to 1955, then V.Herbert, 1957, D.Burt of London, 1958-61, rebuilt after a crash, sold by Chiltern Cars to J.Ruben of South Woodford. The car was then owned by Peter Hodges who with Doug McNeil bought the car from Gordon and Glynn, for a three month tour of Europe in about 1958. Of this tour Doug McNeill recalls the laps around the Nurburgring, the fascination with the car by Ferrari mechanics at Maranello, the traversing of mountain passes, a broken crankshaft between Nice and Monte Carlo (the replacement crank with matching rods and new main bearings were sent out by Gordon and Glynn cost £14). David John Burt then had the car in whose time the luggage racks were photographed - perhaps a remnant from its European tour. (see p45). It was then imported into the USA in 1968 by Frank Heaney. Homer Tsakis bought the car in 1980 and with Richard Mikovitis gave a chassis up restoration replacing timber work as well as bearing replacement and head reconditioning. Richard was tragically killed in a plane crash as the work was completing. The car was exhibited at Hershey. The car returned to the UK sold through Dan Margulies to Mrs Elisabeth Lambert who owned and made good use of the car from 1987 as daily transport and longer trips including bringing the car from Hampshire to the annual Coventry rally each July. She had contact with the widow of Peter Hodges. In 2003 Bramley Garages sold the car via Marryet in Belgium to Hannelore Hipp in Germany who sold it on to the present owner, also in Germany in 2005. The car still carries a screen pillar lamp which was on the car in the 1950s.

Chassis Number   6025513

Photograph at a Coventry Rally- highly original and beautifully prepared.

Original Registration No	WD8853
Date of Registration	19 January 1935
Original Engine No	55144
Gearbox Type	ENV Wilson p/s
Rear Axle details	5.5 ratio, but with intention to fit higher ratio
Body style and type	Standard Imp sports with correct aero screen fittings
Body Colour	BRG with green and black trim
Wheels and Tyres	19" and 18" sets
Trim details	Black weather equipment including side screens

History   Some competition use in the car's first two years. Previous owners include Lionel Boddy, Percy Blamire, a Mr R Oaks of Coventry ('58-'61) and two others. The present owner bought the car in 1963 and spent five years restoring it to its present fine order. Modifications included replacing the $1^{11}/_{16}$" shaft with a Merlin crank, rods were polished and balanced and Omega pistons used with shortened skirts, drilling front and back for weight equalisation. Bores were sleeved back to standard, $1^{1}/_{8}$" twin SUs fitted and oil pump plungers were enlarged to $^{5}/_{8}$" in a phosphor bronze housing. Valves, guides and end caps all made to suit. Braking modifications to the shoes, pulleys fitted with needle roller bearings.   Keeping the central clamp locked gives 60% front 40% rear performance. Use of 18" x 5.00 tyres on the rears is found to give a better ride. On the human side Percy and Gordon Blamire who rebuilt the car in 1943 having purchased it in 1940 for £160 were delighted to be reunited with the car in July 1996 at a Coventry Rally. They noted that stainless steel shackles they had prepared were no longer on the car. Such are details of some memories!

Chassis Number 6025517

An extract from the Riley Record.

Original Registration No	CME 412
Date of Registration	1935
Original Engine No	55110
Gearbox Type	ENV Wilson p/s
Body style and type	Standard Imp Sports
Body Colour	Red ("signal red")
Wheels and Tyres	19" then 18"
Trim details	red upholstery with black (duck) weather equipment

History   Colin Douglas who at the time was working at Connaught's, living in Wimbledon Park, wrote in 1976 that CME 412 had been stolen 6 months after he had bought it in 1954 and no trace has since been made of it. He wrote that "such records as a young racing mechanic kept of his own transport were with the car and the log book has been surrendered. It had been insured with one of the Lloyds syndicates who settled the account at £150. The car had been bought from Dudley Gahagan's garage. Colin recalled it being in standard state though on 18" wheels, scarlet bodywork with red trim including pneumatic seat cushions. He also recalls there were no side screens and about 50,000 miles recorded for its 20 year life. The car is photographed at Starkey's Corner, Donington, driven by A.L.Phillips, (see p. 30). Engine number is in sequence and as listed by the local authority (Greater London Council).records .

114

Chassis Number 6025973

Original Registration No   WS 650
Date of Original Registration   28.6.34
Body Colour   Cream

History   Licensed as 2 seater   Licence cancelled 31,12,58. Last owner Thomas Welch, 40 St Mary Abbots Court London W 14.   Nothing more has emerged .

Chassis Number 6026098

Original Registration No   KV8454
Date of Registration   29 March 1934
Original Engine No   48892

History   Registered in Coventry on 29 March 1934 there is a note, acc to Peter Banner's search of Local Authority records, that this was an experimental car, but scrapped on 24/3/36. The chassis number placed here seems unusual unless the next Imp was also a development exercise. Nothing else known.

Chassis Number 6026133

Photograph by Neville Farquhar 1984

Original Registration No   AHP 545
Date of Registration   17 December 1934
Original Engine No   Acc to the Works Sales register lists 54898
Gearbox Type   Originally ENV, later Silent third gearbox

Body style and type	Was 2+2 now reproduced standard Imp sports body
Body Colour	Early traces of red, then for much of its life, paint free. Now dark green.
Wheels and Tyres	Mid term 17" fronts and 16" rears. Now 19"

Photo by A.N.Farquhar in 1984: N.B. Spring pins in line with cross member and an un-boxed chassis

History Due to its deteriorated state, this car has now been rebuilt to standard Imp format as seen opposite. However a number of important questions remain about its story. The car was registered to and used by Capt Riley in events as a demonstrator in late 1934. It was then sold to Charles Taylor of Borth Dinon St.,Birmingham. Eddie Maher confirmed to Nev and Barbara Farquhar that this was what remained of the 1933 Show protoype, which had been "pushed into a corner and left till someone found a use for it", eventually required for an event, specially prepared and fitted for that with a Works competition engine, all set up and running and registered. Later, Arnold Farrar attested that the car was fitted with the racing crankshaft in an Ulster specification engine with triple plunger oil pump. Previous owners after Taylor, include Bill Brindley, of Codsall, Wolverhampton who ran it in the Land's End Trial in '38, '39, and '46. Brindley was brother in law to W.E.(Ted) Jones who joined Rileys with Hugh Rose to work on the V8 and 15/6 engines, all according to Arnold Farrar. Other owners were Alan Cottam and Bill Hylton. Hylton, in his ownership removed the magneto and drove a distributor from the exhaust camshaft and ran an oil pump from the inlet camshaft. It was bought by Bruce Winder in New Zealand and retained by his widow. Bill believed the original engine to be 54292.

It can be argued that this is the original show car from the 1933 October motor show. (See details page 7). Of course, the chassis number, engine number and date of first

116

registration is as listed in what were Arnold Farrar's sales records and in the Sales Register Farrar lists the car as the prototype MkII Imp with its extended body shape. But its unboxed chassis as illustrated above suggests an earlier date. Its Competition mechanics are accompanied by the competition chassis with front dumb irons and spring mounts in line with the cross member as used on the Ulster Imps.   Farrar's records show it to have been first fitted with an ENV box and claimed it to be the only Imp fitted with Girling brakes from production. These would have been fitted when prepared for competition.   Curiously, the chassis was built of TORMANC steel, to standard dimensions but lighter in consequence.   A Silent 3rd gearbox was a later addition so there are other departures from any original condition. However it did have 2+2 bodywork, up until the recent restoration and it is interesting to compare the photo on page 115 with the show car pictured on page 7. Note also the filler cap in photo on page 115 when compared with the reference to this on page 3.

Bill Brindley took a silver medal in the 1939 Lands End Trial and it was later raced by Alan Cottam between 1955 and 1960 later known for his exploits with his Connaught.

AHP 545 now in New Zealand and rebuilt into standard Imp form

The 6027 Series cars

Chassis Number 6027230

From the Goddard Collection by kind permission, photographed in the 1960s

Original Registration No	GC 2675
Date of Registration	Not known, the reg'n no being transferred from a 1930 car of unknown make
Original Engine No	Not known – now quoted 197156
Gearbox Type	All Helical manual. Stamped 24.10.33 D 41
Rear Axle details	5.25:1 M 25344
Body style and type	Standard Imp sports
Body Colour	Tartan red, Was Bugatti blue
Wheels and Tyres	19"
Trim details	Black

History previous owners include J.C.Butler of Tadworth in '61 Russell Wilson Kitchen who in his 5000 miles with the car claimed he got through 3 crank shafts and much money! Other owners include J.H.Davidson ('72), Derek Swann, and Dan Margulies who sold the car to a now long standing Swiss owner. It has won many Concours awards in the recent past. The car is fitted with All Helical gearbox, perhaps as original but with the flexible gear selector linkage system, so this, or the box itself may be a later alteration. In an extensive rebuild in the early 1980s by Ian Gladstone at Blue Diamond Services, the block was replaced owing to cracks in the original. The windscreen is now to standard.

118

Chassis Number 6027305

Photo of Sarah Rheault's Imp whilst on the New England 1000 Event in May 2007

Original Registration No	AON 434
Date of Registration	20 February 1935
Original Engine No	55518 now with a 12/4 engine 35-3094
Gearbox Type	ENV Wilson p/s
Body style and type	Standard Imp
Body Colour	Was green, painted maroon later, in USA
Wheels and Tyres	18" and 19" were Silver now body colour
Trim details	Was brown, then black now brown again

History The present owners in the USA bought the car from a Kensington dealer while in the UK, the previous owner being a Mr A Jones of Edmonton, London from August 1964. Chiltern Cars (their sales folio no 1391) noted engine no 5518 when it was with them putting it in sequence with other engine numbers. Engine no 53094 has also been listed for this car. After crankshaft breakages over five years Jones fitted a 12/4 engine with an early type Sprite head and inlet cam with twin 1¼" SU carburetters. The cable brakes were also converted to Girling rod type. Used in competition in USA where it was taken in 1973 by the then owner the next year passing the car to his wife who has used it competitively on circuits including Limerock and in Hill Climbs in the USA. The leather upholstery has been restored back to the original brown.

Chassis Number 6027310

Under the Judges eye at an early 'Coventry' (An ANF Photo)

Original Registration No	JM 4370
Date of Registration	1935 First Registered in Jersey
	Registered in England 25 March 1939
Original Engine No	55508
Gearbox Type	ENV Wilson P/s
Body style and type	Standard Imp sports
Body Colour	Maroon with red Upholstery
Wheels and Tyres	19" now, previously 18".
Trim details	Black weather equipment

History The first owner of this car and its registration number in Jersey remain unknown. The other previous owners are E.J..Laker of Cranleigh from 1951 who used the car in trials (see pages 34 & 35). In 1955 it took part in the VSCC Jubilee at Goodwood Then with G.E.Weaver of Stourbridge and to W.D.J..Lamb of Brierley Hill, West Midlands, from 1965 who won a number of Concours events. Charles Cross purchased the car in 1983 the car remaining in Lincolnshire, then passing to the present owner in 2004 who has had a good deal of work to do to bring it back to good order in that the car had deteriorated during its time laid up in the intervening years. Featured in the American hardback: Automobile Quarterly - vol 9 no 1 in 1970. Original weather equipment is with the car.

Chassis Number 6027324

Original Registration No	X7275
Date of Registration	1 April 1935
Original Engine No	55500.
Gearbox Type	ENV Wilson p/s

History Car last known in Sri Lanka undergoing restoration.

Chassis Number 6027335

Original Registration No	Not known
Current Registration	WXW 988, previously O22 (Australia)
Original Engine No	12/4 unit currently fitted no 37-5724
Gearbox Preselector,	A/S, originally ENV 75 no R551
Bodywork	Standard Imp Dk Green
Trim	Red pleated seating, black weather equipment
Wheels	Silver, 4.50x19 tyres

121

History This car moved from the UK to New South Wales within 2 years of production, and was race prepared by Arthur Rizzo, a then well known Riley tuner but racing was accompanied by various engine blow-ups. Rizzo preferred the 12/4 and fitted the engine and gearbox from a Falcon. Bill Clayton bought it post war and raced it, notably at Bathurst in the 1950s,and had it in general use. Damaged in an accident it was left "under a peach tree" for up to 15 years. Well known it was taken on by Geoff Baker who ran it fitting new front wings, & repairing the radiator, but with the scars still visible today, then selling it to Paul Baee, he owning it for 12 years. The present owner wishes to convert it back to a '9' and has engine no 47626 and an ENV box R551 all in preparation.

Chassis Number 6027351

The car part restored at a Coventry Riley Register Rally

Original Registration No	CXU 569
Date of Registration	14 July 1936, acc to a previous owner
Original Engine No	55520
Gearbox Type	ENV Wilson p/s

History Previous owners include a Mr Shortland, who described the car as having four Amal carbs, and hydraulic brakes and having been black, blue, ivory and maroon and who stripped it and re-sprayed it black. In 1961 it was with M.Margetts of Guildford and in 1965 it was sold to a Mr Kennedy of Luton, and to H.D. Marsh of Newark from 1966 in whose time the body was black with red upholstery and red side screens and weather equipment. Tony Hough of Melton Mowbray then had it for a time, selling it on to the present owner who has carried out a major restoration.

Chassis Number 6027359

Photograph taken of J.P.Hill with son Joe aboard, on Adderstone Hairpin on the London-Edinburgh trial in 1938, said to be demonstrating the eternal validity of Newton's Laws of Motion

Original Registration No	OW 7859
Date of Registration	November 7 1935
Original Engine No	55514
Gearbox Type	Manual box
Body style and type	Standard Imp Sports
Body Colour	Originally red, now Grey with green trim

History The car was trialled pre-war by J.P.Hill who (acc to Ian Hall), later trialled the Sprite ABA525 which later went to Wilson Nicholson. The son of 'JPH' – A.H.Hill - known as Joe(!) - continued the interest but the next part of this Imp's story is not known. The current owner's father bought the car in July 1964, from D.J.Webster of Lytham St Annes, the mileage reading 54,000.

Worthy of study overleaf are the line drawings used for promoting the miniature model of this car featured in "Prototype Parade No 146" q.v., ("Model Cars" 1964), the work of A. Russell Black. The car carries an MPH style spare wheel rear cover but lacks the centre vertical rib fitted to those cars. Two other Imps recorded carry these plain covers. (See chassis nos 6024868 and 6025048). Incorrectly shown are an over-slung rear chassis frame and this mistake has recurred on other miniatures. The manual gearbox shown is as fitted to the car, though the front wing curve is over accentuated. The seating is twin bucket rather than bench type: perhaps this was used and to good effect in trials such as that shown above! Twin horns are mounted below headlamps and an auxiliary driving lamp. The real car has been slowly undergoing a major restoration. The car is believed to have had Girling brakes from new.

123

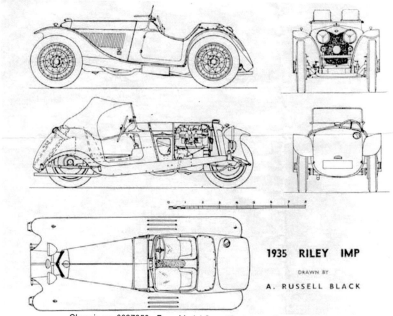

1935 RILEY IMP

DRAWN BY

A. RUSSELL BLACK

Chassis no 6027359, From Model Cars "Prototypes Parade", 1964.

Chassis Number 6027360

Photographed at a Coventry rally when car had been imported back into the UK

Original Registration No   BRR 222a, (Australia). Now DSL 721
Date of Registration   1934
Original Engine No   55785   Now 43479
Gearbox Type   ENV Wilson p/s gears quoted as
15.4, 9.2, 6.6, 5.0:1
Rear Axle details   5:1
Body style and type   Standard Imp Sports body
Body Colour   Red with red trim, was white in the 1980s
Wheels and Tyres   4.50x19" Colour red
Trim details   Black weather equipment

History   Previous owners in Australia include Lance Dixon, Peter Briese, and Jim Runciman, to 1998 when a major rebuild and restoration was carried out in 1990/91 by Noel Wyatt. The car now in UK, the owner lives in Warwickshire. To accommodate the taller driver, (Jim Runciman is 6'3"...), the cross bar at the seat rear has been moved back while the gear quadrant and selectors are mounted on the transmission behind the gearbox, after the style of the MG K3 Magnette. (Visible in the photo). Twin SU carburetters are $1^{1}/_{8}$" The car is currently very active in VSCC and Inter Register speed and rally events.

Chassis Number 6027369

Photo taken at a recent Coventry Rally

Original Registration No   JK 4454
Date of Registration   13 March 1935
Original Engine No   55804
Gearbox Type   ENV Wilson p/s R2032 HR
Rear Axle No   M25720
Body style and type   Standard Imp Sports
Body Colour   British Racing Green
Wheels and Tyres   19" Coloured silver
Trim details   Fawn, no sidescreens

History Known in Putney in 1966, the present owner bought the car as a 'barn find' in 1970 from Tom Lane in the Dorking area. A previous owner was a naval officer and it is thought that the car spent some time in Italy, perhaps in that connection, the national badge being mounted on the radiator and which has never been removed. A 'full keeper history' with the help of DVLA is being pursued. A nut and bolt rebuild was completed in the 1970s and the car has continued to have extensive use along with its MPH stable mate

Chassis Number 6027370

Photograph during the ownership of Michael Gardiner - note the high mounted wipers

Original Registration No	AJH 531 (Jersey in the 1970s as 11945)
Date of Registration	6th April 1935
Original Engine No	55844, Various now Merlin M2954
Gearbox Type	Manual - Silent Third.
Body style and type	Standard Imp Sports
Body Colour	Black
Wheels and Tyres	Cream colour, 19"
Trim details	Red upholstery and beige weather equipm't

History Tony Chipp recalls the full screen with top - mounted & central pivots as shown. Bought in 1957 from Willow Garages Somerset he drove it home to the Midlands on his motorcycle licence. Then to L.G.Firman of Silverton, Essex in 1958, Derek Roscoe of Kirkbean from 1971, Michael Gardiner of Stamford, Lincs., Dan Margulies, D.J.Johnson of Sevenoaks who carried out a major restoration, describing the car as being 'in museum condition'. Jamie Doggart, Guensey brought the car to the Coventry Rally in 1984 celebrating the 50th anniversary of the Imp model. It was sold on by David Royle, then later to the Bernie Ecclestone collection of Sports and Racing cars in 1994. It sold for £67,100 in 2007. One previous owner is claimed to have lost his eyesight but so loved driving the car that his wife would take him to a disused airfield where he would drive the car responding to her promptings of left and right! The car has Scintilla magneto ignition. The Gearbox selector extension did baulk the brake adjusters when last seen and the car had no fan fitted.

Chassis Number 6027405

Photo taken at the Riley Register Rally Coventry 2006

Original Registration No   BUW 904
Date of Original Registration 16th March 1935
Original Engine No   55842, currently 42392
Gearbox Type   ENV Type 75 No R1986 HR 28.10.34
Body style and type   Restored to standard
Body Colour   Was Light Metallic Blue with dark blue trim
                                now white with Black trim

History. Letters from Rileys in 1951 about his car to Hugh Langrishe (who was close friend to Ron Flockhart and assisted during his ownership of ERA R4D), set out performance data. The car was sold by him in 1952 to T.Rex Young of Coombe Lane Bristol. This car's licence had lapsed in 30.6.59 whilst in the ownership of J.C. ('Buster') Thompson of Lee, London S.E.12. The car had been owned by Charles Mortimer and featured in <u>Motor Sport</u> in 1956 under the title, "Cars I have Owned", then by R.A.Hassell of Keynsham, Surrey. 'Buster' Thompson was knocked over by a bus and was accordingly compensated. He did a deal with an Alfa/WASH special to buy this car in April 1958 from Performance Cars. He, with his brother Peter, removed the engine with a view to fitting a Big 4 (2½ Litre) for competition work and began to convert the brakes to hydraulic but at each stage did not progress. The car remained largely dismantled till the current owner bought it, minus its radiator but otherwise complete, after a lengthy period of negotiation. Photos of this period show the car near complete but in very poor state. A detailed restoration was carried out by Jim Rose who fitted the Marchal headlamps. After restoration in great detail it was offered for sale in 2007. The car may have been red at one stage but the use of light blue metallic paint was revealed as original, as the restoration of this part-dismantled but otherwise original and untouched car progressed. This use of this type of paint may be another Riley first, in common with 6027685 (qv.).

Chassis Number 6027413

No photograph available

Original Registration No	BVR 15
Date of Registration	30 March 1935
Original Engine No	55890
Gearbox Type	ENV Wilson p/s
Body style and type	Standard Imp sports
Body Colour	Black with red trim
Wheels and Tyres	Rears 16"

History   This car was bought in 1957 by a student from Michael Reed of Brentwood in Essex, who was to take it to Ireland. Described as having wide rear wheel rims, black with maroon upholstery and black weather equipment and in good condition. Previous owners include John Delves who replaced the block. A previous owner using the car for hill climbing had "taken too much off the block" and blown head gaskets resulted. Delves sold the car when the universal joint became due for repair. Burville had the car which was then sold to Mrs V Fraser who enjoyed it but sold it. She later asked Burville to try to recover it for her but instead he sold her AYK 597. John Dixon of Keighley was probably the next owner. Then Colin Ford bought the car in 1962. The car suffered a broken crank. He confirmed the small size wheels and colours but over the years there has been further deterioration. On Colin's death the car will stay in the family. A major mechanical and body rebuild is intended.

Chassis Number 6027414

Photo from an earlier Riley Register Bulletin

Original Registration No	VH7503
Date of Registration	11 March 1935
Original Engine No	55892
Gearbox Type	ENV Wilson p/s
Body style and type	Standard Imp sports, dismantled
Body Colour	Green with dark blue trim
Wheels and Tyres	Stove enamelled silver 19"
Trim details	Black weather equipment

History The car was trialled pre-war with successive entries in the 1935, and 1936 RSAC Scottish Rally, driven by Miss Freda Walker. She married to become Mrs Freda Elliott and ran again in this event in '37 and 38. Her husband Keith Elliott drove the Sprite BFG 1 which she also drove, as also AKV 218. Acc to Cowbourne, *(British Rally Drivers and Their Cars, pub Smith Settle)*, Miss Walker in the '36 and '38 RSAC,was an entry by the Womens' Automobile Sports Association, (see p 33). In 1946 it took part in a Finchampstead motoring event. The present owner was told by his predecessor that Maton raced it post war at Brands Hatch (No 11 is with the car) and elsewhere. He had acquired the car from London Road Garage, North Cheam and who had kept it from 31.12.46 to 30.6.54. In 1948 it was seen wearing cycle front wings. Bob Maton knew Arnold Farrar who had with mechanic Billy Whitsun helped him fit a Merlin Crank. In 1949 the car ran at Prescott on 22 May as entry no 9 and recorded a best time of 62.24 secs. Signs of its competition use include the mounted aero screen. The original log book was destroyed by Huddersfield C.B.C. The present owner rescued the car in May 1973 and at the time of writing, the rebuild of this important Imp is steadily progressing.

Miss Walker in action on the 1936 RSAC Scottish rally. (©Montague Motor Museum)

129

Chassis Number   6027421

Photograph by Nev Farquhar when this Imp won outright the VSCC Oulton Park Concurs in 1965. It was parked between the TT Sprite AVC 20, and the Imp AKV216

Original Registration No	ARW 491 Re registered as 400 MPA
Date of Registration	14 March 1935
Original Engine No	55900
Gearbox Type	ENV Wilson p/s
Body style and type	Standard Imp
Body Colour	Dark Red

History   Early reference to the car is as a demonstrator for Jack Hobbs of Willesden Lane, London. (Source: Arnold Farrar/Sales Log). The registration number was re-assigned in March 1960 through Surrey County Council. Previous owners include Dudley Palmer from 1954, Graham Thorpe of Middlesbrough. Thorpe won the 1965 VSCC Concours at Oulton Park with this car as above. It then went to the USA, where owners included Alexander Mason, Jerome Morici from 1986, Stanley Weiss of New York from 1990, and Tom Fair of Warwick, Rhode Island. It returned to the UK, and was for sale in VSCC Newsletter by F Boothby of Hampshire for £26,500 in 1996.

Chassis Number   6027430

Victor Cromie's Imp (left) alongside Sarah Rheault's at a VSCCA meeting

Original Registration No	BNW 51
Date of Registration	1935
Original Engine No	55902
Gearbox Type	Type 75, ENV Wilson p/s
Body style and type	Standard Imp Sports
Body Colour	White with blue wings and bonnet top.
Wheels and Tyres	19" Colour ivory

History In the mid 1960s this car was in Lancashire, then in Ellesmere Port for three years and was bought in the UK by the present owner who took it to Massachusetts in 1978 after mechanical restoration work had been done by Dick Batho. It is equipped with twin zenith carbs, has a bolted up clutch and has been used extensively in Hill Climbs sprints and races. The oft heard comment in VSCCA circles he quotes as "a very pretty car, quick on corners even on ordinary tires".

Chassis Number 6027431

photograph by Mark Gibbons

Original Registration No	JV3506
Date of Registration	30 March 1935
Original Engine No	55904
Gearbox Type	ENV Wilson p/s
Body style and type	Standard Imp sports
Body Colour	Blue with red upholstery,
Wheels and Tyres	Silver. 19"
Trim.	Black weather equipment

History   First owner was Charles Richard Bascomb of Grimsby, Lincs, then, Rowland Smith of London NW3, next Walter P. Maidens who trialled the car, (see opposite) Louis Boschetti of Harrow in 1949, Malcolm J. Edwards of Harrow in 1959 and thence to the USA from 1968   where Mark Gibbons bought it from Philip Barbour of Stanford Connecticut. He used it in competition in hill climbs and races.   In 1991 the car passed to a new owner in Hyannis. MA. USA.

From Riley Record in 1941, "An 'Edinburgh' Memory,- W.P.Maidens coming through the Gateway, Gattonside" pre war. The car is wearing the badge of the British Monte Carlo Competitors Club (noted by Ian Hall).

133

Chassis Number 6027432

Following restoration work by the present owner. Note twin Zenith carburetters

Original Registration No	BXL 550
Date of Registration	27 March 1935
Original Engine No	55912
Gearbox Type	ENV Wilson Type 75, p/s
Body style and type	Standard Imp Sports
Body Colour	Green and silver (see below), then Red with black trim, now dark Blue with biscuit trim
Wheels and Tyres	19" dark blue colour

History Twin Zenith Carbs and a now incomplete 'Jackall' system. Previous owners include film star Rosamund John, later married to John Silkin, T.D.Marshall (in N.Ireland) , & Peter Roberts who did a major restoration in the mid 1980s. It changed hands to a Shropshire owner in 2003.

A Riley Record Photo of Rosamund John with husband and young John Howard.
She starred in "The way to the Stars", "The first of the Few", and other films

Chassis Number   6027433

Photograph extract from an Australian magazine

Original Registration No	RR 076 (Australian) KRH 182 and UE 255
Date of Registration	1935
Original Engine No	55910
Gearbox Type	ENV Wilson preselector with bolted up clutch
Body style and type	Standard Imp Sports
Body Colour	Bright red, Black upholstery and hood
Wheels and Tyres	White, 19" 18", 16" used in competition,

History   Bill Dick (first owner when it was Bugatti blue). Believed to have spent all its life in Australia. Previous owners include Richard O'Dwyer, bought in Ballarat who had many Rileys, then Geoff Harrison from November 1969 winning Concours events including the VSCCA in 1972. Then back to Bill Dick when the car won 'best in show' at the Ballarat Classic Car show. Entered also in the state Concours at Wattle Park in Melbourne in 1979. Now in Launceston Motor Museum.

Chassis Number 6027438

135

Original Registration No	APT 590
Date of Registration	14 April 1935
Original Engine No	55938
Gearbox Type	ENV Wilson p/s
Body style and type	Standard Imp Sports
Body Colour	Was Red with red upholstery, now blue with dark blue trim. Black hood and sidescreens
Wheels and Tyres	19" were yellow, now dark blue

History   Previous owners include Donald Perera from 1953, G.M.Preston from 1955, Brian P. Clarke also in 1955, A.J.Hill in 1955, Raymond Fenwick from 1965 D.Mewes, from 1974 with whom it spent some time in Bern, Switzerland where it was put up for sale. Ron Phoenix purchased the car from Harold Webb of Chelmsford in whose time and since it has featured on birthday cards and calendars. For many years it has been housed in the Ulster Transport Museum prior to which Ron used it in competition on the Mandello circuit near Dublin, the Kirkistown circuit, and in hill climbs at Craigantlet, Cairncastle, Croft, and Ennisbury near Dublin, many of which are longer than the equivalent hills used in England. It competed at Shelsley Walsh at the Vintage meeting July 10 1983. It passed to a new local owner on Ron's death.

Chassis Number 6027439

Photograph taken by Mary Simpkins during an Alpine tour – twin spares fitted here

Original Registration No	BYY 575
Date of Registration	8 August 1935
Original Engine No	55936, Block stamped 25.7.34
Gearbox Type	ENV Type 75, no R2001HR 1.11.34
Rear Axle details	5.25:1 IMP M25798
Body style and type	Standard Imp Sports
Body Colour	Was Maroon, but Connaught Green since 1958

Wheels and Tyres	4.50x 19. fronts, 4.75x19 rears
	Maroon, then silver now Connaught green
Trim details	Was maroon, now tan. Tan hood & Tonneau

History   First owner Henry Moss (of Moss Empire Theatres) who had Hydro-telecontrols fitted and who took the car around the Nurburgring in 1936. Bill Symonds had it from 1936 and loved it and drove it again in May 1994. Subsequent owners included Padgett, Steele, Mortimer, Joseph Mayo from 1948 to 1952 who bought it in Manchester. His son Paul has kept contact with the car. In his father's time the car had 4 Amal carbs, a 4 branch exhaust, and an ex Dixon High Compression Imp head, that he had obtained from Victor Gillow which it still has. It had quite a high mileage then. Mike Spence had the car from 1958, (Formula 1 Lotus works driver, killed at Indianapolis in 1966 in the Chaparral). He made some modifications locating the gear quadrant on the rear of the gearbox, fitted a solid drive in place of the centrifugal clutch, fitted bucket seats, and 16" rears and painted it dark green. Lamps are fully chromed. John Gathercole bought It in 1962, relocating the Quadrant and restoring the original seating layout. The Scintilla Magneto was rebuilt by Bosch for £6-10s including carriage. The ENV box was rebuilt by Bill Morris in 1991 and a Merlin crank rods and Hepolite pistons fitted. The car has been used regularly since 1979 in VSCC and Inter Register speed events, driving tests and many navigational rallies, (including some Measham Rallies) with various awards. It has also taken the Maher Muller award at the Riley Register's national Rally. Touring has included Scottish tours, including one honeymoon, parts of France, the Alpine passes, the Pyrenean foothills, and the Italian Lakes. It is featured extensively in Graham Robson's book 'Riley Sports Cars 1926-1938' published by Haynes.

Hood arrangements. Photo mid 1980s. This car has side screen drillings in the door frame (as do many others), but none are fitted. Not all cars have this drilling.

137

Chassis number   6027447

Photograph taken by the present owner soon after acquisition showing Girling fittings

Original Registration No	BYK 947
Date of Registration	11 July 1935
Original Engine No	55950
Gearbox Type	All Helical Gearbox but now fitted with ENV.
Body style and type	Standard Imp Sports
Body Colour	Red with red trim
Wheels and Tyres	Silver, 19"

History The car has Girling Brakes (fitted by Burville) and modified headlamps with inserts. The present owners bought it in 1969 in partially stripped state from a Mr Hamilton Smith. Having other Rileys the major restoration has been delayed but the car is now back in use. In the 1960s the car belonged to Gerry Dick who used it in competition.

The car now restored and road worthy, 2006

138

Chassis Number 6027462

Photos by kind permission Noel Wyatt

Original Registration No	BXM 820 (UK). First Registered in Australia NW138 now registered BXM820 (Australia)
Date of original registration	8 April 1935
Original Engine No	55960
Gearbox Type	ENV Wilson Type 75 No R1988HR, 30.10.34
Rear Axle details	5.25:1 but now 4.89:1
Body style and type	Standard Imp Sports
Body Colour	Believed light blue before red, now dark blue
Wheels and Tyres	19" (4.50 x 19) all round having been 16" wheels all round when purchased in 1982
Trim details	Interior dark blue, Black weather equipment

History   The car was sold into Switzerland around 1963, then to A.J.M. Van der Loff in Holland in 1971. At this time Ewout Bezemer saw the car and noted it had Scintilla magneto and twin Zenith carbs, was dark purple in colour and on 16" wheels. Dashboard and lighting were then non standard. Returning to Margulies, the car then went to Australia in 1982 where it eventually underwent a major mechanical and body restoration to original specification by its present owner. This included fitting twin SU carbs but later reverting to the original Zenith carbs. The car is used extensively. The photo below helpfully details the gearbox and central braking system.

Chassis Number 6027477*

Photograph circa 1980 at Riley Register rally Coventry

Original Registration No	Not known, earliest recorded 892 RMC re-registered ADU301 in the 1970's
Date of Registration	1958
Original Engine No	None.
Gearbox Type	Was fitted with ENV type 75 p/s, later manual Silent Third replaced this,
Rear Axle details	5:1Components used ex a Saloon
Body style and type	Sporting 2 seater, Ulster-styled lines
Body Colour	Pale blue
Wheels and Tyres	18" front 17" rears, cream colour

History *This Imp chassis has a number adopted from a car no longer in existence. Essential details are as follows. A used Imp chassis with road springs and other fittings was bought for Gerry Groves as a 21st birthday gift in 1952. It was built up by him as an Imp Special but he sold in 1957. It was first registered in 1958 as 892RMC. The next known owner, in 1965 David W.G.Miller of Cambridge, described it as having a very agricultural body but photos from Groves and Millar prove continuity. When Miller sold the car he retained the engine and a Silent Third gearbox. It was then acquired by David Styles, at that time in Sutton Coldfield. M.A Shearn bought the car from Styles c 1971 as an engineless rolling chassis inclusive of a new body (built by Ferguson of Nailsworth, Glos.). He sold it to the Bradfords in 1972 with further work waiting to be done. It appears in the Riley Register's membership list in 1980. The engine fitted was a special series Nine, together with a type 75 ENV gearbox and hydraulic brakes. The Ferguson body had a pointed tail and louvred style bonnet. Shearn used chassis number 6027711 in the absence of any other number but this was never verified. Richard Bradford had the car after this and did significant work, sorting it to the condition seen above. He changed the gearbox and had the engine prepared by Nev Farquhar, and work to the body by Peter Woodley.

An ENV box was with the car, later to be replaced by Bradford for Silent Third. As the car had not been licensed for some time, in 1981 the Local Vehicle Licensing Office stated that the records of 892 RMC had all been destroyed. There did however remain a tax disc of this registration attached to the remains of the first body. By this time the car had gained the plate ADU 301, released, to the surprise of many, by the Coventry Licensing Authority, it being an important number among Works cars' histories. In addition, in the absence of a proven chassis no., the chassis number 6025035 (q.v.), thought to have been defunct by now, had also been adopted in view of the uncertainties surrounding this chassis' origins. This was the situation when the chassis 6025035 was found in South Africa with enough of its original parts in circulation to allow that car to be reconstructed. The car was sold on to Paul Jaye and on to Dan Margulies. Correspondence was conducted with one London Ferrari specialist, who had this car for sale listed as an Ulster Imp, and at the same time with the Licensing Authority at Swansea to set out the record of these two cars which shared the same identifying numbers while being visibly different and separately identifiable. This car has changed hands since these events spending some time in the UK, used in competition by Duncan Sutton, then in Germany and in the USA. Recently Coys promoted the sale (their picture below), stating a chassis number of 6027477 but still with ADU 301 as the Registration number. If both or either of these cars arrive back in the UK at the same time to claim this number, DVLA will have to address the matter...

Circa mid 1960s as 892RMC

Coys copyright - sales photograph 2003 reproduced by kind permission.
Standard front spring mounts visible.

141

Chassis Number 6027484

Photograph illustrates the front spring mounts on the standard Imp

Original Registration No	BXO 32
Date of Registration	20 May 1935
Original Engine No	56014
Gearbox Type	ENV Wilson p/s
Body style and type	Restored Standard Imp Sports
Body Colour	Dark red. With beige trim and black hooding
Wheels and Tyres	19". Colour matching dark red

History   This Imp has coil and distributor ignition. So far, K.F.Rouse is the earliest known owner in 1948. Graham Galliers (well known for current exploits at Shelsley Walsh), acquired the car, probably in 1971 and restored it, including wings, running boards (which were missing), and upholstery to correct specification. At that stage the car was white and cream and on 18" front wheels and 16" rears. Galliers noted that the car had been maroon, originally. Subsequent owner was Tony Smith of Cheshire in whose time the ENV gearbox was rebuilt by Bill Morris with new bands, and needle roller bearings replacing the bronze bushes. Other mechanical work was done to brakes and oil pump. The car was sold in October 2005 and again in July 2006 and now lives happily in France. Its present owner fulfilled a lifelong ambition to own an Imp, having been £15 short of a possible purchase of such a car in 1953. He writes, "Later in life I moved into Ferraris, having a Dino for twenty years. But with those cars now rather common and not the car for Rural France, I can indulge myself with my first love in the years left to me."

Coil and distributor Ignition and standard fitting of 1" SUs. The two breather points on the engine are visible but rarely seem sufficient. The fitting of 1 1/8" carbs on these cars attracts but is often ineffective, pistons not opening fully due both to weight and vacuum requirement. A drip tray is often provided by owners to avoid neat petrol dripping on to the electrical controls at the base of the steering column! The single SU pump in this position is standard. Note the 'hot spot' manifold. The short fan mounting unique to the Imp can also be seen.

Chassis Number 6027493

John Rolls with his wife in 1955 on holiday in Devon in their Imp (Family album photo)

Original Registration No	BAU 519
Date of Registration	18 April 1935
Original Engine No	56022
Gearbox Type	ENV type 75 No. R2018 HR
Body style and type	Standard imp sports
Body Colour	Originally Green, but now Bugatti blue,
Trim	Black upholstery
Wheels and Tyres	19" colour silver

History   Previous owners include J.K.Roberts ('58) P.K.Shaw of Essex in 1961 and John Roberts later owned BGP530.   John Rolls bought this car in 1955, the summer of '56 spent in a major body-off repaint to leaf green with Brunswick green wings. Sold to a man in Weybridge on command of his Sales Director, (who deemed the car unsuited to his position and occupation!), seen again for sale in '64 in New Cross, London, in sad state and then red, given a test run but was aggrieved at its deteriorated state. Then to Cyril Bradford, and J.A. Burke (of Rocky River, Ohio) from 1968, who carried out a near total rebuild of the car at considerable expense, including timber framing as well as mechanical repair and restoration. In 1988, John Rolls called on Barrie Gillies to view one that was for sale only to find BAU 519 was on offer. To drive it a few yards and hear again the sound of the gearbox reawakened the past. The deal was done with Chris Drake Collectors Cars, who were the selling agents, paying 80 times what he had sold it for, even re-mortgaging the house. It is now Bugatti blue with light blue wheels and much work outstanding from its time in USA and many detailed parts missing but restoration has begun. The owner lives in Berkshire.

Chassis Number 6027496

Photographed in 2003, prior to rebuild

Original Registration No	WG3688
Date of Registration	7 May 1935
Original Engine No	56020
Gearbox Type	ENV Type 75 No 2019, date 13.11.34
Body style and type	Standard Imp Sports
Body Colour	Black with red upholstery
Wheels and Tyres	19", colour silver grey

History For some years this car was exhibited in the Birmingham Science Museum during the present long ownership since 1963. The car currently features square rocker boxes, coil ignition, twin trumpet horns, triple wipers and greasers on the axle trunnions, and a four branch exhaust. The dashboard is $^1/_8$" alloy plate. Interesting original trim and seating were retained until 2002. The first owner was Charles Sleigh who was an entrant in the RSAC rally in 1935 (entry no 54), (See page 33).) Then Peter Riley who also ran an MPH at one stage and who married Ann Wisdom, daughter of Tommy and 'Bill' Wisdom. Peter Riley went on to class wins at Le Mans, Nurburgring, Mille Miglia, and was a Works Healey, Works Ford Zephyr and Works Sunbeam Tiger driver, an ace rally man. The car also passed through the hands of Chiltern Cars in 1953, and in 1961 to Dawsons of Staines. The hood frame mounting and use of space behind the seat squab (see overleaf) illustrate the original arrangement. The hood frame will unfold to the vertical, it then locks with steel tags securing it to bear the hood under tension. In 2004 a major refurbishment was carried out by Jim and Bruce Young. During this restoration the body work, was found to have holes indicating competition use and the fitting of event plates. A fine painting by Peter Griffin of this car appeared in <u>CAR</u> magazine in 1966.

Behind the seating the original hood arrangements and fold up shelf/support

146

Chassis Number 6027497

Stephen Harvey examining this Imp example in 2006

Original Registration No	ARO 451
Date of Registration	25 June 1935
Original Engine No	56042 but now Merlin
Gearbox Type	ENV Type 75
Body style and type	Original Standard Imp Sports
Body Colour	Cream with green wings, had been all green
Wheels and Tyres	Cream 19"
Trim details	Dark green

History This two tone finish in 1935 would have cost an extra £5 . The engine now uses a Merlin block with oil filter, but with square rocker boxes. A worm and sector steering box is fitted. Post war SUs are fitted without adaptors to a Brooklands type manifold. Front brake levers have been lengthened by welding and pulley settings adjusted accordingly. Twin horns (trumpet type) fitted. The car is believed to have raced at Boreham in the 1950s, the brake modifications mentioned having some bearing on this. It was owned by Duley Palmer of Esher in about 1953. Other previous owners include P.B.Heath from April 1967. The car was mechanically rebuilt by Gordon Middleton prior to the owners move to the Yorkshire coast. The work was eventually completed at 3am, the car then driven there by Gordon, who having finally put up the hood found the horizontal snow blew in one side of the car and out of the other. The car is now in Leicestershire. Overleaf are additional pictures of the hood and seat arrangements as also shown on p 146

Another original hood frame: arrangements with small shelf, hinged and fitted to rear of seat. This shelf rests on the shallow lower section of the parcel shelf. The starting handle has also made its home here!

148

Chassis Number 6027562

"Minor work needed ...."

Original Registration No	First registered in Australia, probably 438855
Date of Registration	1935
Original Engine No	Has both 56530 in sequence and 54694
Gearbox Type	An All Helical box has replaced the ENV
Body Colour	Originally blue, now green with silver wheels

History   This car entered in the Australian GP in 1936 on a handicap of 36 minutes but failed to start. The original owner, Dan O'Leary, fitted four Amals and an external water manifold on the exhaust side below the head to cool the valves. Multiple Carbs were shielded by a perforated panel let into the o.s louvres, these were still with the car in Alby Lobb's workshop in 1978. A refrigerator engineer, O'Leary also made up the dashboard, removed the wings replacing them with cycle wings. The headlamp mountings were not to standard. He sold the car to Ira Phillips, who had a major accident when the steering was lost, the drop arm ball joint coming apart and the car passing through a wire fence. Luckily for the driver the wire caught on the radiator cap, which was damaged and replaced! Via a dealer it went on to E.A.Hillman and then R.L.(Roly) Forss. Curiously, Forss had seen an Imp in a crash with the Glenelg tram, managing to put it off the rails. He later bought the car in the 1950s, without knowing its past but discovered the reality when finding repairs and new metal welded in to the chassis The car would not run as the inlet cam was very worn but the lobes were re-built with stellite. It was fitted at that time with a water pump driven from the camshaft and the bottom hose point for the radiator on the opposite (off) side to standard Imps. The car had been cream with red wheels and red trim. Many layers of paint overlaid its original blue. It was raced extensively post-war by Forss including the Collingrove Hill Climb. It passed to Albert Lobb then on his death to Neville Webb, then to Jim Runciman, who bought it from Adelaide in tatty condition (acc to present owner).

149

The car had a pointed rear tail fitted at one stage held on by over centre clips, "as fitted to Ulster Imps". The Ulster body shape differs from the standard Imp, with a flatter top and squarer shoulders while the sloping tail continues to a flat floor. The type of tail, possibly the actual tail described may now be with Ch No 6027665. (qv)., as the tail was later passed to another Imp. There is pre-war racing film of the car running off the road in a race at Lobethal, wearing the pointed tail. The fuel filler was extended to pass through this tail panel. Previously a different dashboard had a large central rev counter. The ENV box was replaced by an All Helical box in the1950s. The current owner set about a total restoration from its dis-assembled state which was completed with major assistance from Noel Wyatt who replaced the wings and dashboard to original styling and had to make up new parts that were missing.

".......to complete" *(Photos Noel Wyatt)*

Chassis Number 6027563

Photograph taken after nut and bolt restoration by the owner in the 1980s

150

Original Registration No	GUP 385v now IMP934
Date of Registration	not known
Original Engine No	56348
Gearbox Type	ENV. no 2023 HR
Body style and type	Standard Imp sports
Body Colour	Dark Green with green upholstery
Wheels and Tyres	18" Green colour

History. This car may have been owned by Tom Luxton (see p174), later featured in the Australian Motor Manual, Jan 1st 1959 in a curious comparison with the 2 stroke Berkeley having been restored by Bob Nicholson during the ownership of Peter Nicholls, then having a centrally placed ENV gear quadrant, then to Ron Brownrigg. Owned since 1965 by (the late) Mr Barrie, and then Mrs Rosalind Scott. Rosalind is the daughter of Percy Riley. Hydraulic brakes were fitted at one stage but the cable system has been re-instated. (See ref in the Foreword to this book).

Chassis Number 6027627

Photograph taken at Montlhery 1999

Original Registration No	BXV 671 currently BPK472 Berlin
Date of Registration	1935
Original Engine No	56312
Gearbox Type	ENV
Body style and type	Standard Imp Sports body
Body Colour	Was Red with Beige leather work
Wheels and Tyres	19", 4.50x19" Colour Burgundy
Trim details	Black weather equipment, no side screens

History Previous owners include A Richardson of Sands,Bucks, Miss J.L.Fraser (daughter of Mrs V Fraser, see p 50 &128), who bought the car from Stanley Burville, and Michael Hetman who has owned the car since 1982, when it was overhauled by Ian Gladstone of Blue Diamond Services.

151

It was then driven back to Berlin. It broke down half way across East Germany and had to be towed some distance to Berlin. There was only minor difficulty with the East German Police (in the DDR at that time), but the trip caused the serious undoing of the gearbox. The ENV requires that if the car is ever towed over any considerable distance, top gear must be engaged so that both oil pumps in the box are running. Better now, it is well used on continental touring, including 4 times to Montlhery, also to Scotland and Ireland. (See page 45).

On tour in mixed company, somewhere in Scotland – the only way to see the view

Chassis Number 6027633

Original Registration No	BYY 909
Date of Registration	Not known
Original Engine No	56316. But Merlin Engine currently fitted
Gearbox Type	ENV No R 1997 HR
Body style and type	Standard Imp Sports
Body Colour	White with black leather upholstery
Wheels and Tyres	19" and 17" used colour silver
Trim details	Black duck hooding

History Had not been used for about 20 years in the Birrell's ownership. The upholstery and dashboard thought not to be original. The screen has more rounded corners than the original. Previous owners include Calthorpe who once worked for Freddie Dixon, and had the car in S. America and transferred it by an epic journey from Argentina to Chile (See Riley Register Bulletin issues 112 &113, 1984). George M. Birrell bought the car for £425 from Mercury motors of Wembley following a total rebuild – even the brake pulleys were bright untarnished brass! Such was the condition that he was loathe to use it as an every day car but shortly afterselling, bought it back for his sister Miss HT Birrell who used it intensively between Ruislip and Oxford, Then it passed to William J.Birrell, then to Ivor Halbert. George Birrell recalls "blissful handling, a gearbox ridiculously ill suited to the distinctly cammy engine and less than thrilling acceleration, which became of no importance when you could find clear road and could forget the brake pedal, an endearing car." Ivor Halbert found fitting 17" wheels x 550 tyres gave a better ride, though the rear end hopped about a good deal on corners. He had the ENV box rebuilt by Bill Morris who fitted more appropriate ratios and he fitted a Merlin engine using the heavier crank though the original one remains with the car.

153

Chassis Number 6027638

Photograph taken by Dennis White

Original Registration No	BXO 31
Date of Registration	20 May 1935
Original Engine No	Not known, now 62722
Gearbox Type	ENV Type 75 no R 1989 HR
Body style and type	Standard sports body
Body Colour	Apple green with black trim
Wheels and Tyres	Silver 4.50x 19

History This Imp was featured in the article by Herbert Euston in Autocar 1943. It was bought in 1994 by Dennis White of Crewkerne, after a 30 year lay up in poor condition, on 16" wheels, he having looked at 12 Imps before making a purchase. He carried out a total restoration in the mid 1990s. Notable is the existence of BXO 32, (6027484) demonstrating the sluggish sales pattern in the mid '30s, presumably registered on the same day perhaps by the same dealer albeit separated by 191 other chassis and 7 other Imps!

Chassis Number 6027664

Photograph taken by Arthur Hilliard

Original Registration No	not known
Date of Registration	not known
Original Engine No	56404
Gearbox Type	Now uses type 150 Armstrong Siddeley P/s
Body style and type	Modified
Body Colour	White with black trim
Wheels and Tyres	Silver
Trim details	Black

History The Myers brothers of Victoria intended to use the frame of this car with a Bristol engine but this never happened. The body was used in the Downing Replica (qv). According to letters from Jim Cahill to Gerry Murphy, the then owner of the "Downing Replica", the chassis, engine and preselector gearbox were sold to Arthur Hilliard. The Downing car used a newly created lightweight chassis and lightened components. There was also a sister car created with heavier frame. On to the original Imp frame, Mr Hilliard built up a racing Special fitted with a 2½ litre post war Riley engine. A Roots blower was also used giving 14-16 p.s.i. boost and the whole geared to 28mph per 1000 rpm. To withstand the loading the diagonal cross bracing was fully boxed and the 2.5 litre unit was fixed at either end of the block, in pursuit of additional stiffness. Later stages of the story were the fitting of an Autovia engine mated to an ENV type 150 preselector gearbox. The car passed to Arthur's son on his death and continues today.

Chassis Number 6027665

Ch No 6027665 wearing tail extension

Original Registration No	(Australia), unknown, EGS 381 in 1971.
Date of Registration	not known EGS381 (1971) Then 011 now
Original Engine No	56406 [33433H
Gearbox Type	Originally ENV, now Silent 3rd box.
Body style and type	Standard Imp Sports
Body Colour	Dark Green with tan trim
Wheels	17" Silver

155

History : Brought out of storage in 1946 and often referred to as an Ulster Imp, Steve Power raced the car post war at the Lowood track in S. Australia and who fitted a very beneficial under-shield and claimed an increase of an extra 10 mph to a max of 105. Royce Jutner had the car from him to 1955, then to Michael Robinson. The car was restored for another owner by Kevin Delbridge, a Sydney based producer of Speed equipment, who, so taken with the car he was rebuilding, offered to purchase it, which the owner accepted. He in turn raced it, mainly at Warwick Farm race track. One race, in Sept 1966, was marred by the oil gauge line fracturing to empty its contents on him. He made up the 4 SU manifold seen here. The car has a 2 gallon electron sump, an Ulster water pump, feeds the radiator to its off side, forged spring eyes, electron nosepiece and many other Ulster features with a Lucas magneto, a 4.77:1 final drive and detachable "Ulster style" tail. See note on 6027562 re these tails.

Chassis no 6027665,with four SUs on the special type manifold, built up by Delbridge, and visible Lucas Magneto and Ulster water pump

Chassis Number 6027667

No photo available

Original Registration No   AUO 347
Date of Registration   June 11, 1935
Original Engine No   56406
Gearbox Type   ENV

History   Little known but this car was last owned by Michael John Rushin, 39 West Street, Portchester, Hants and the last licence expired on Sept 30th 1961, certified by Devon Co. Council on 8th Jan 1965. The previous owner was a Mr Thain of Chichester in '59 and before him, Cyril Price who bought the car in 1957 from Dennis Stenning of Reading when it had 16" rear wheels and 18" fronts with 5.00 tyres. The clutch had been bolted up. Cyril described the car as inordinately quick, holding MG PBs at bay and quicker than his next Imp KV 8932. Cyril unlocked the clutch and reinstated the centrifugal mechanism buying all the necessary bits from Jimmy James of Castelnau, Barnes. Sadly this only made the car slower off the mark and heavier. It was changed for a 3 litre Bentley! The car had Ace wheel discs which enveloped the spoked area of the 18" wheels: four long bolts from the inner plate, screw into a cast ring on the outer around the hub, the outer main plate then being screwed on to the casting with a C spanner. The outer plate was polished alloy.

Chassis Number 6027668

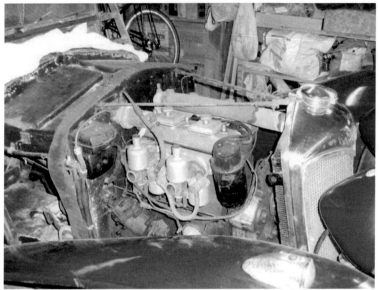

Beauty is in the eyes of the beholder. Note the reversed head, and earlier rocker boxes

Original Registration No   CUU 285, later R88 and MJ 88
Date of Registration   March 28 1936, Confirmed by Chiltern
Original Engine No   56416. Chiltern records confirm this.
Gearbox Type   ENV
Body style and type   Standard sports body
Body Colour   Maroon with beige upholstery
Wheels and Tyres   18" colour aluminium

History   This car is fitted with Girling rod brakes and the suggestion has been made these were original to this car. Some cars were to special order and the later date might agree with this, though the car falls in the main chassis sequence. The first owner was DFW Parish, Batchelors Club, South Audley St W1. Later in 1940 it was bought for Cameron Millar as a 21st Birthday present. This succeeded a Lea-Francis which had in turn replaced an Austin 7. He had joined the RAF at 18 and flew Whitleys and Halifaxes and was involved in a daylight raid on the Scharnhorst. His Imp was sold on by him in 1956 to purchase a 3 litre Sunbeam in which he came to specialise along with 250F Maseratis and he assisted significantly in the film Monte Carlo or Bust.[41]   Later this Imp was owned by Dr P.J.Grey, who claimed 'Ulster' tuning for the car. Thence to Renton, Ellman-Brown, who bought the car in 1970, then to Peter Le Couter. The car now has a new owner in Coventry who is carrying out a thorough restoration. A picture of this Imp graced one edition of the Batsford book, "The Sports Car" by John Stanford, a cover that caught many eyes. Present at 1955 VSCC Jubilee, Goodwood when still in the hands of Cameron Millar.

---

[41] See The Vintage Sports Car Club Bulletin Issue 243 Spring 2004 p 66. I am indebted to Alan Lomas for this detail who was in touch with Cameron Millar through those times.

Chassis No 6027673

Original Registration No	DMP 520
Date of Registration	1 April 1936
Original Engine No	56442 but now fitted with a Merlin unit
Gearbox Type	ENV preselector, type 75
Body style and type	Standard Imp sports on a new frame
Body Colour	Bright red with black upholstery.
Wheels and Tyres	19" 4.75/500x 19 tyres, wheels painted black

History Previous owners include Molly O'Neill, Lugham. J.H. Bagley a master at Uppingham School, and during whose ownership Barbara Farquhar drove this car on several occasions. After V. Basil, Fred Aran, of Northampton owned it from 1957 but was tragically killed in a motor cycling accident. Then to Bill Symons, of Otterburn from 1972, Herb Schofield, from 1983, who had the body reskinned with extensive new timbers by Peter Chapman. Sold in 1983 by Coys in Birmingham, it then went to Graham White, and on to a new owner in Berkshire. By this time it was found to have serious chassis rot and Barry Gillies was commissioned to build a new frame for the car. The car has cable brakes, (see further on 6027668), and carries a screen pillar lamp. and in 1973 had an MPH - style spare wheel cover. The car is featured on the front cover of Dr David Styles book, "Rileys the Forgotten champions" (pub by Dalton Watson).

Molly O'Neill here driving her Imp in the Liverpool Motor Club 1952 Speke Driving Tests
(A dual entry was for husband Garry) At this time the front wings looked permanently surprised about
something, here also wearing smaller lamps. (the photo by Frankie Penn and published in Autocar)

158

Chassis Number 6027674

Photo taken during John Hoehn's ownership

Original Registration No	FV 6310
Date of Registration	31 July 1935
Original Engine No	56412
Gearbox Type	ENV Wilson p/s
Body style and type	Standard Imp Sports
Body Colour	Was white also black, now burgundy
Wheels and Tyres	19", colour Silver
Trim details	Dark red leather. Weather equipment black with red beading

History Previous owners include Mrs Sophia Handley (first owner), of Umston, Lancs, D.E.R.Tutin '58, Cyril Harding, from 1958, Jack Fisher of Barrow in Furness, Christopher Mann from 1963, T.H.Gadsby from 1964, W.G.Davies, from Vintage Autos of London from 1965 and who took the car to Canada. It has gained various Concours successes. J.W.Hoehn Switzerland bought it from Dan Margulies. By Hoehn's time the headlamps were stepped down to 7" sealed beam units, but later re-instated, the dash board was skinned in black leather and the Hobson telegauge removed, adjustable seats fitted, "Sprite" style, the arched member behind the seats was removed to allow adjustment. In 1974 Jack Bond had bought the car from T.H.Gadsby but took a long time to sell it as so many prospective customers found they could not get in it!

Chassis Number 6027675

Now in the ownership pf Sr Ravetta: opposite is a photo taken in the 1960s in Barry Dukes ownership

Original Registration	CLD 597, now MIF 96361 (Italy)
Date of Registration	1 March 1936
Original Engine No	56450
Gearbox Type	ENV preselector
Body style and type	Standard sports with round wing valances
Colour	Originally dark red with dark blue trim

History   There are a number of Imps which have a rounded valance in the style of MG wings. One advantage being claimed that the weather performance is better, and less risk of corrosion. Previous owners include Ransome and Barry Dukes who modified the wings to this style to improve spray control in the wet. He took the car on an alpine rally, meeting an Italian who begged to purchase the car to which Barry eventually agreed: Gianni Mortarotti later sold it to Roberto Ravetta near Pavia, Italy.

Chassis Number 6027676

A timeless photograph taken by David Wood in Scotland in the 1970s

Original Registration No CNW 213
Date of Registration 14 August 1935
Original Engine No 56408. The car later has a Merlin unit
Body style and type Standard sports
Body Colour Believed black with red upholstery
Wheels and Tyres 19" Silver
Trim details Black hood and tonneau

History A Mr S. Hornby took delivery of this Imp on 19th August 1935, but was offered no choice of colour (black with red trim) or gearbox (pre-selector), getting the feeling that this was the end of the line! He sold it in Sept 1936 but repurchased it in March 1947. He then rebuilt the engine and fitted 18" wheels in place of the 19" supplied and had it painted a light blue but with increase in the family sold it again in 1949. He writes that Rileys did fit one Imp to overcome its lack of luggage space with an odd shaped case that went behind the seat covered in leather cloth to match the trim. He did offer it to the last known owner – an unusual prize! Previous owners also include David Wood of Worcestershire, who toured extensively with it but later selling it (in 1964 for £365), for something more suited to travelling to site meetings with attendant equipment in all conditions. The car was last known to be in Essex, "stripped for rebuild". Telescopic shock absorbers have been fitted at some stage.

The Imps of Peter Banner, David Wood and Barry Dukes in mutual admiration in the late 1960s

Chassis Number 6027677

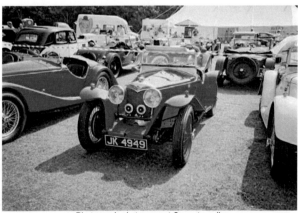

Photographed at a recent Coventry rally

161

Original Registration No	JK 4949
Date of Registration	21 August 1935
Original Engine No	56420
Gearbox Type	ENV type 75 R 2024 HR
Rear Axle details	M26035
Body style and type	Standard Imp Sports
Body Colour	Was Dark Green, then light blue
	then dark red, now red
Wheels and Tyres	19" x 4.50 Centre lock (was 19" / 16").
	Were Black, now red
Trim details	were missing recently, now dark red

History Rob Dean writes, "I finally found a photo of my Dad during the war in the Riley he owned for a very short time, he bought it off a Rolls-Royce rep and it cost him £75 which was a huge amount then and a few months later the guy he bought it off came to him and said he had made a mistake and could he buy it back. Well Dad couldn't really afford it and so he sold it back to him. The reg number was JK 4949 it would be fun to see if it was still around and Dad had a nice picture of it in front of some Blenheim Bombers". For a time in the Melville Smith collection, other owners include Peter Harper(a Warrington dealer) in 1971 who bought the car from Dan Margulies. Then to Ralph Mingay, in whose time it lacked a well for the Spare in 1974. Les Keeling bought this car in 1982 in dismantled state and restored it, the chassis and axles were rebuilt, as was the ENV gearbox. The engine was sleeved back to standard. The body required some re-timber framing and this was done by Nick Jarvis and by T.Buckley of Oldham. Mouldings on the doors were fitted and the dashboard put back to original pattern. Then to T.F.Watson, then R Murphy of Dubai in 2003. For sale via Keith Pointing in April 2006, the car is now in Kent.

*In the ownership of Rob Dean's father (here riding passenger) and in full WWII trim
in the company of Blenheims*

Chassis Number 6027678

Another Imp with flying connections – this time Squadron Leader Neville Duke photo c 2002.

Original Registration No	BRA 763
Date of Registration	June 29th 1935 (Derbyshire)
Original Engine No	56430 with twin Zenith carburetters
Gearbox Type	ENV
Body style and type	Standard Imp Sports
Body Colour	Believed originally black, now BRG
Wheels and Tyres	19" Silver
Trim details	Believed originally brown now tan

History   Currently owned by d'Lisa Simmons of USA but kept in the UK. Neville Duke, WWII ace and test pilot for Hawker Siddeley, owned this car in 1946 just before his marriage to Gwen when they changed to a Sprite - which she particularly liked. She recalls that as he was now holder of the world Air Speed Record and representing the Hawker Company with frequent receptions at the Ritz he was under pressure from Hawkers to drive a more 'respectable' car. The Sprite was in use throughout his record attempts. He sold the Imp to a Napier Engine Company rep in Luton. Bill Ashton next from 1950 who overturned the car causing minor damage. He acquired a Brooklands and sold the Imp to friend Bill (W.C.) Blake of Shoreham, Sussex who did an engine overhaul and fitted oversize pistons after a rebore. Bruce Beattie probably the next owner, broke the crank in Cheddar Gorge. In the re-build some Imp engine parts disappeared, Stanley Burville having the car at that point. Robert Eley Cooper of London W.8., then bought the car in 1957 selling on to Chiltern Cars. The car was then used in UK and France by d'Lisa's father thence to the USA, losing its registration number. With ENV trouble, a general rebuild was embarked on in about 1960 by d'Lisa Simmons' father and completed by her both there and back in the UK with much help from Mike McQuire and Allen Clear. TSJ 731 was provided as a UK number, but BRA 763 was eventually recovered.

Sqdn Leader Neville Duke, & his wife Gwen with the current owner (photos M.McQuire)

Chassis Number 6027679

Original Registration No	BYV 466
Date of Registration	23 August 1935 (Middx)
Original Engine No	56432, now with Carillo rods & Sprite timing
Gearbox Type	ENV Type 75 No R2006HR
Rear Axle details	5:1 but now fitted with post war 4.89:1
Body style and type	Standard sports, Black as original, had been white

Wheels and Tyres   Lighter green
Trim   Green leather, Black weather equipment

History Previous owners include G.J.W. Moncrieff first owner who ran it in the 1936 Monte Carlo Rally with co-driver R. Serjeantson, (See Motor Jan 1936), and in trials pre-war. R. Woodhouse Wild from 19.3.46, who created the pointed tail and raced at Boreham Then L.J.Bailey in 1954, J.I.Morris in 1955, acquired for the present owner in March 1960, on his 21st birthday, with cycle wings and the modified tail. The doors were faired in. The wings were happily retrieved. In the long rebuild which followed the correct tail was restored with new framing and panelling. At this time Reece cams were fitted and a special crank to Merlin standard.

Chassis Number 6027680

Henrik Schou-Nielsen at Fanø Beach Races, 1994 prior to recent restoration

Original Registration No   Unknown DVLA: SSV 336, now K 35 336
Date of Registration   Unknown
Original Engine No   545553, now fitted with Sprite engine
Gearbox Type   Pre-selector, but Silent 3rd fitted 1994
Wheels and Tyres   were 19", as now with twin spares

History: Believed originally exported to Holland with twin spares, metric instruments: speedo in km and fuel in litres. Longer rear wings to comply with local laws. Previous owners include Willy Oosten, from 1948, who raced at Zandvoort. Rallies include Tulip, Evian Mont Blanc, Mont Ventoux, Alpine etc. Much modified during 1950-52. Oosten fitted the 1½ litre engine and 18" wheels from his Kestrel Sprite which "rendered the Kestrel a sheep in Wolf's clothing". In consequence of the modifying works the car gained weight to 975 kgs, (19cwt), but remained competitive throughout the 50s and early 60s. (See page 34). Film and many photos remain of this time. Sold in 1966 to the furniture designer Poul Kjaerholm in Denmark, loaned to the Bonfils brothers till the gearbox gave up in 1974. Into storage, then bought by Henrik Schou-Nielsen from Poul's widow in 1984. Restoration work was begun in 1994 including the fitting of a Silent 3rd gearbox and standard rear wings. Further full restoration in 2007 completed, the Oosten engine awaits work. The car has had extensive use in the last 10 years, retaining the Sprite engine and with 19" twin spares.

Chassis Number 6027681

This Imp during its long period of storage prior to its current rebuild programme

Original Registration No	AKV 443
Date of Registration	12 September 1935
Original Engine No	56434
Gearbox Type	Originally p/s but crash box from c1938
Rear Axle details	5:1 fitted later in place of 5.25:1
Body Colour	Green with green trim
Wheels and Tyres	19"

History Owners include W.S.Gibson from Sept 1935, then to Rugby area, Martin Rich from 1949 H.Bayley, on the Isle of Wight from 24.2.53 who bought it from Chiltern Cars, T.J.Peerless from Feb 1965, Mrs T.J.Peerless. Sold by Bonhams in Sept 2007, the car is now being restored in the Devon area by its new owner. W.S.Gibson in The Autocar 28.1.44, in their 'talking of sports cars' series said he fitted the crash box and 5:1 rear axle and changed the Zeniths to twin SU's and noted that the car ran at above 90° and had an oil temp gauge which showed 60° hot. The centrifugal clutch absorbed much power and only disengaged at 300rpm which on a tuned engine meant it was permanently engaged. The photo below shows the car during Martin Rich's ownership dating from about 1949, note the late twin horns and correct wing forms although Gibson had fitted MG J type wings in his time. The photo below shows the car before Angela and Martin Rich were married. Taken in about 1949. At that stage according to Angela there was another girl in the car....

AKV 443 in the late 1940s.

Chassis Number 6027682

Photograph taken by David Wood circa 1960

Original Registration No	not known, later 512 JTU in Cheshire in 1960 and AXF651 in Sweden.
Date of Registration	1935
Original Engine No	extant 50984
Gearbox Type	ENV Type 75
Body style and type	Standard Sports
Wheels and Tyres	18"

History From a plate on the dashboard the car came from a dealer in Larne, Northern Ireland. Subsequent owners include S. Bournville, Peter Saul, in'61, John Le Sarge, then via Dan Margulies, the car having a broken crank. The car then went to Sweden, to Thore Lewin, and then to Dr Hans Larsson. Between Bournville and Le Sarge, an owner in 1971 noted the car being fitted with friction dampers with hydraulic controls. These were replaced with original dampers. He commented that the bonnet shape indicated the fitting of a supercharger at some point and that axle parts had been plated. The centrifugal clutch had been discarded and the ENV bands used in its place. He raced the car at Silverstone. A Merlin crank had been fitted. He enjoyed 25,000 miles of trouble free motoring, but records do not say who he was!

The car in the ownership of Hans Larsson

167

Chassis Number 6027683

Photograph taken during Dr R.J.R. Llewis ownership circa 1970

Original Registration No	CMV 91
Date of Registration	20 September 1935
Original Engine No	56420, then 47252
Gearbox Type	ENV Wilson p/s
Body style and type	Standard Imp Sports
Body Colour	Red with red and black upholstery
Wheels and Tyres	19" were silver colour now red
Trim details	Black weather equipment

History   Previous owners include Harry Rose & Co Ltd of Hendon being the first registered owner, later Mr Stokes of Eton Garage, D.J.Sizer of Somersham Hunts., Maurice G.Reeve-Black, & Dr R.J.R Lewis in 1963 who reconditioned the car, Fuad Mazjub, Barry Price who rebuilt the engine following a loose flywheel, then to Erica Pilkington who used the car extensively in VSCC events. In 2006 it passed via dealerships into France where it is in regular use.

Chassis Number 6027685

Celebrating 50 yrs of owner enjoyment – Alan Lomas' Imp in August 2005

Original Registration No	AKV 216
Date of Registration	1 August 1935
Original Engine No	56448 with twin Zenith carburetters. Car originally had saloon timing settings.
Gearbox Type	ENV type 75
Body style and type	Standard Imp sports
Body Colour	was Black then in 1937 to metalescent light blue/green.
Wheels and Tyres	19" 4.50 front 4.75 rears, now 4.00 front – fits the spare well and gives lighter steering.
Trim details	original green with duck hooding

History Previous owners include Philip Francis Kent 1935; J.Greenwood, Todmorden, 1936; W..Arnold dealer, Manchester 1936; Mr Marshall, 1937, Manchester; Hebden Bros, Burnley; Ratcliffe and Thornton, Nelson; Bambers, Southport, all dealers, during 1937/8, then in 1938 to Daniel Heib of Greenmount, Bury, the present owner buying it from him in 1955.– perhaps the longest ownership of any Imp and featuring a notoriously sweet sounding engine. It featured in "The Picture Story of World Sports Cars" by Stuart Seager p 63 pub 1965. Also featured in Mark Gillies book "The Golden age of the Riley Motor Car" pp 36-37. Due to porosity the twin Zeniths have been replaced by twin $1^1/_8$" SUs and cams reprofiled to Sprite timing, but lacking any other modern 'mods', still uses among other things its 3-Brush dynamo. The paintwork finish, being an early pre-war refinishing in 1937, is often a cause of discussion but there is at least one other example of use of this paint type pre-war on another Imp (see also Ch no 6027405). The backs of panels on this car often have "104" pencilled on them, coming close to the numbers of Imps in this listing, This list is not comprehensive. But it raises a question and other owners might check for similar markings.

169

Chassis Number 6027686

Undergoing major restoration

Original Registration No	Not known but 1952 DLI -2152 Delhi
Date of Registration	1936 (Quoted Yr of manufacture)
Original Engine No	No. 56452 but later Merlin engine fitted
Gearbox Type	ENV

History According to the present owner's researches, this car was supplied to India, the first owner being the daughter of an English ambassador in New Delhi or Calcutta. It was later owned by a Mr Pretap Roy during the 1950s and 1960s. The ownership then passes to a Mr Bertil Weinborn and a Mr Arvid Weinborn followed by a Mr P.V.Billgren. It was last taxed in India in 1971, after which time it was sold to a Mr Hans Hauben, a German diplomat who took the car with him when he moved from India to Mozambique. He then sold the car to Lief Lindquist who was then working in Mozambique and employed by Saab-Scania. After considerable difficulties about both purchase and export, he took the car with him when he returned to Sweden in 1989 . When it finally rolled out of its container, tyres and wiring had all been eaten by rats! Later that year it was sold to the present owner. Calcutta Registration papers dating from 1970 verify some of this history. A modern dynamo conversion resulted in a bulge in the bonnet.

Chassis Number 6027752

Photograph Sept 1966 during Ron Brownrigg's ownership. 2-Twin choke SUs and Scintilla Magneto. Note the standard Imp chassis[42], and hydraulic brakes.

Original Registration No	Not known, currently ZZ660
Date of Registration	Not known
Original Engine No	not known, now a 12/4
Gearbox Type	P/S
Body style and type	Standard Imp body style Dark Green
Wheels and Tyres	White,

History   This could be the last Imp produced. The chassis number source for this car is as quoted in Riley Register correspondence. The chassis is standard Imp form but with the gearbox point cross member moved back 4" to accommodate the 12/4 unit and the cockpit bridge member removed to allow for driving position. Two twin choke SU carburetters have been fitted with Scintilla magneto ignition. Owners include McReady, Kurt Schultz and Ron Brownrigg who acquired the car in 1959 and fitting the 12/4 engine   eventually claimed   a 13.5:1 compression ratio giving 135bhp, gaining a number of successes in competition in Victoria and at Mallala in South Australia. A lap record at Warwick Farm, was never to be broken. Brakes were also converted to hydraulic. Other substantial modifications made and in this state of tune the car was timed at Sandown, Victoria achieving a standing quarter mile in 14 secs. Ron sold the car in 1967 but bought it back again in the early '70s, but stripping it for development was as far as things went. In 1995 the present owner, in the Sydney area,   Stephen Figgis, acquired the car from him, when it underwent a complete rebuild, and now has the car in regular use. It was recently featured in a major article in an Australian car restoration magazine and ran at the 2005 Collingrove Hill Climb in South Australia.

---

[42] See p. 17

Imps with chassis numbers not known

Reg no GX 731 J.S.Maitland in Australia, a well known car, but with chassis number not known, details unconfirmed

Original Registration	Possibly GX731
Date of Registration	Not known
Original Engine No	Not known
Gearbox type	ENV
Body style and type	Standard Imp sports
Body colour	light Green
Wheels and Tyres	17" x 5.00

History This car was driven into 3rd place in the 1936 Australian Grand Prix on the rough Philip Island circuit. In 1958 John Holley drove it in the ASCC 1100cc Hill Climb championship. It was featured in Sports Car World in 1955. The car has twin $1^{1}/_{8}$" SU carburettors and a Scintilla magneto, cooling is by thermo siphon. Dick Russell used the car in trials and light competition work before it was sold to the present owner who has owned it for many years.

The Brooke special

The Brooke Special in recent form. (photo - Geoffrey Perfect)

Henry Leslie Brooke (Brookie to his friends) served his apprenticeship on motorbikes. Later as a driver he competed at home, Indianapolis; and extensively on the Continent. Racing with the greats; Fangio, Ascari, Villorese, he was the first English man to win an international Grand Prix in Belgium after the war. He took part in two Mille Miglias, five Monte Carlos, Le Mans and practically every GP in Europe. He was also awarded the George Medal for his saving work during the Coventry Blitz. To the unknowing a Coventry car breaker, he fitted an 1100cc MG Magnette engine into a 'slightly bent' Imp frame he was offered, to build a racing special, to mark his exit from motor cycle racing. The car was to be blown. To this, Riley axles and brakes were added. A Riley gearbox was mated through a special flywheel and clutch. IFS followed and other major changes to the frame. Much modified throughout, the car today runs with a 2 litre ERA engine fed by 6 SUs and a new body by Barry Gillies.

173

Australian Imp – GL 249

This car is probably chassis no 6027563 one of the Imps long domiciled in Australia and listed in the profiles in the earlier part of the book. But as Registration numbers change with relocation it is not easy to identify which chassis is at work here! So who has Tom Luxton's car today – probably Rosalind Scott.

Ean McDowell writes: "This is Tom Luxton in his Imp in about 1947. The photo with planes in the background is on Ballarat Airstrip in 1946 or 47, the first motor race meeting held in Australia after the war. "

"The other photo is on Geelong Road, now a 6 lane highway to the largest provincial city outside Melbourne but in those days still a gravel road judging by the dust. The story was that the AVSCC held a sprint meeting early in the morning before the police were out and about. I am amazed how the driver's hat would stay on and in the original I think you can just make out that he was smoking a pipe." Note the design of the side-screens.

The Densham Special – YX1967

Photograph taken in 1949 at the Riley Works Durbar avenue. Perhaps the Company should have taken on production of this one? They considered it according to John Densham.

History Pre-war, John Densham (a Riley Apprentice) from 1935 built up a special based on a vintage chassis and fitted a racing body, ex works, from the then current Ulster series. Reg No YX1964. The car has a racing crank $1^1/_8$ " carbs, and a 4.66 CWP – ex Brooklands. The body could have come from one of the dismantled TT cars, nothing is proven. A lighter Brooklands body (from scrap - such were the days!) was later used. Various Cozette blowers (Ex FN), were tried and Scintilla Vertex and BTH magnetos with differing timing chests. In 1946 he then acquired from the works a standard Imp frame, presumably a spare, as the only marking found is D100, n/s and forward of the engine mounting, put there and later verified by Densham himself. He built on to it the parts from the pre-war special with the addition of an all enveloping body as pictured above. Chassis and parts were acquired by Stephen Harvey from Jack McEwen who had it for a time. Henry Geary (contemporary at Riley's) suggested that D1, D2 etc might indicate dismantled cars but this is a guess. The car is being newly constructed to conform closely to the pre-war body on the Imp chassis.

The vintage frame to Densham's recipe but with the ex works body, modified to have doors mounted. Body features common to the Ulster format but different fuel tank.

175

Chassis Number not known

Original Registration no BPL 1 seen here taking part in the 1935 RAC Rally which ended at Eastbourne. See page 33. Driven by C.V.Wells. Photo from Robson 'Riley Sports Cars' (© LAT Photographic). Another photo page 201.

Chassis Number not known

Photograph from Riley Record of Hector Dobbs in the 1935 (Jan) Exeter Trial awaiting the start on Harcombe Hill.

Reg no OW 5506 or perhaps DW 5506. OW 5506 is now on a well known 1935 Kestrel, a Southampton Registration mark where Dobbs was a Riley dealer at Hedge End, Southampton. (With thanks to Ian Hall)

The 'Wagstaffe' Special

Photo by Ray Moriarty at the time of the sale of parts. Front of frame – straight cross member, but the structure above the second cross member leaves us guessing.

Photo by Ray Moriarty: rear of frame

History   This assemblage of parts came up for sale with the death of Claude Wagstaffe in 2004. He had been building a collection, according to those who knew him well: some came from Cuth Harrison, Bob Gerard and elsewhere and those in the know awaited with interest to see what might emerge. Sadly his death intervened. Rodney Green bought these parts and with other helps has constructed a special, Imp chassis-based with many Ulster parts to his own preferences. The unmarked Imp frame, was acquired by Wagstaffe from Ross Stokes of Chiltern Cars, traded for other parts, and has front spring mounts in line with the front cross tube conforming to Ulster Imp arrangement and the springs have forged eyes, so the chassis might have originally have had competition intentions or use. The structure above the secondary cross bar has been removed in the rebuild. Has twin plug head, twin spark BTH Mag, Silent 3rd CR gearbox. Rear of the chassis extended beyond the rear cross member at the time of sale. Rear axle mountings are competition type but it seems Wagstaffe planned studs not U bolts. The CWP housing is electron, 5:1 ratio. A special body is fitted.

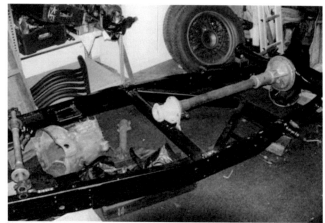

Photo by Ray Moriarty- note Silent 3rd gearbox, Ulster torque tube & alloy nose piece.

Rodney Green's completion of the Wagstaffe project – a lower body line than an Ulster

178

Chassis Number not known

Photo from Allan White Collection

Car first registered as BLD 733, London Oct, Nov or Dec. 1934

Photograph taken of BLD 733   at Filton in 1940. This is Flying Officer Michael E.A.Royce whose brother W.B.Royce was also in the same squadron: 504 (auxiliary) Squadron (Hurricanes). Happily, both men survived the war.

There may be subsequent use of this car in trials by Cyril Corbishly from Macclesfield who was later highly successful in Trials and Rallies, according to Ian Hall. Here it is one of the few Imps seen with Solex carbs and side screens.

Chassis Number not known

Photo from 'Wheels at Speed' Prince Chula © G.T.Foulis & Co Ltd

Original Registration No. BLL 170 issued by London late 1934

History Bira's standard car and chassis which, after Thomson and Taylor had breathed on it, had an improved top speed of 87mph. The car believed broken up and no trace of its existence as researched by his niece. See also page 30.

Photo from 'Wheels at Speed' Prince Chula ©G.T.Foulis & Co Ltd

Chassis Number not known

Photograph: Riley promotion

Reg no APU 200

History   Works Demonstrator may have only been used briefly. Featured in Riley Record. This registration now belongs on a 34 Kestrel. See also note above on OW 5506, page 176.

Chassis Number not known

Registration no CMV 511
Photograph taken in Ireland at Donebate, 1937/8 of an Imp with radiator modifications taken from a Triumph Dolomite! The car is also noted as supercharged. (Ulster Vintage Car Club news sheet) Nothing more known.

181

Chassis Number not known

Original Registration no CGH 353. In the Harrow Car Club on the Wimpey's Estate, South Harrow in March 1936. B.A.Leigh in 'The Maze'. Leigh put up the best performance of the day. (Item in <u>The Light Car</u>). Probably a 1936 registration.

Chassis No. not known : Car was in New Zealand

Photographed in Auckland new Zealand in 1936: a lady visited New Zealand by way of Australia and drove this car from Auckland to Wellington, intending to ship it back by train. Hearing of this, intrepid Arthur Dexter regarding that as a waste of a good car and a good drive (and whose wife and child are in the photo) he took the train to Wellington and drove back to Auckland in 11½ hours - a significantly fast time, roads then being what they were. No details are available of this car's identity.

Chassis Number not known

Reg No CGH 400

Photograph taken of Mr J.B.Ashton during the 1937 MCC Lands End Trial. He went on to get a Silver award. This will be a late '35 or even '36 registration.   (© 'Ferret' photo, by kind permission).

Nothing else known of this car, curiously another car with CGH Registration – see previous page.

Of the following cars nothing more is known:

Reg No XNU 298   Derbyshire County Council certified this car to have been broken up, the last issue of a licence being 30th June 1959, and the last owner was John Sutcliffe of 138 Rochdale Road, Firgrove, Rochdale, Lancs. But it is also listed against the name A.R.Breeze, Macclesfield Jan 1960.

Reg No WN 4070 or may be 7040 Registered Swansea later 1934

Reg no CXU 89 London Registered circa May 1936

Reg no KV 5086. History: Nothing known about this one. It may have been the registration number mounted on the original show car in 1933, according to a David Styles suggestion in *"As Old as the Industry"*.

Reg No LRO 797 Late 1950s belonged to David Miller

The 'Cheltenham' chassis. A part chassis had been spotted stored for many years in a mews garage to the rear of Pittville Crescent Lane, Cheltenham and was rescued by Clive Blissett for £7.10shillings in 1968 where it had been for many years after an accident. Clive writes of this one: 'The front section from the scuttle forward was discarded and an attempt made to attach a front chassis from a Plus Ultra @1933. How the chassis came to be in Cheltenham I know not. It appeared to have been in the mews garage for many years prior to 1968. Presumably the accident took place in the mid '50s. The chassis was sold on in 1999…to a Wiltshire member together with a coil ignition 9 engine, a "double top" gearbox, back axle less the short torque tube which found its way into Phil Longhurst's trials car. A 1965 registration disc came with the chassis.'   This registration no is '892 RMC' and associated with the chassis of the car bearing Ch. No. 6027477(q.v.) which continued in use till the early 1980s on that reg. no. Since that time, the whereabouts of the part chassis also remains an untraced mystery.

The Downing Replica

The body from chassis number 6027664, when other parts were sold on, was fitted to a reproduction lightweight chassis prepared for racing. Many lightened parts were also used and the car had some successes. The Downings were Minerva agents in Brisbane becoming Riley agents from 1929 and purchased this Imp body with all fittings from the Myers brothers of Ballarat in 1952. It had a high spec, a double gear 'booster oil pump driven off the rear of the inlet camshaft and an extra oil tank between the dumb irons, four Amal carbs and a manual box with Brooklands shift and Girling rod brakes, hydraulic assisted. Wheels are six stud bolt on. The car well known in Australia as the Downing Replica remains in Queensland. (A Noel Wyatt Photo)

Copies of Imps (the sincerest form of flattery?)

A number of new chassis frames have been made in recent years and have combined with predominantly original Riley parts. This has created a number of imitation Imps both in the UK, Australia and elsewhere. Other copies have been made using adapted and modified chassis from other contemporary Riley models. One such, based mainly on 1936 Merlin parts and adhering closely to Imp specification is registered JK6309.

Blue Diamond Services had a batch of frames produced by Mike Lucas and were stamped BDS and numbered from 1 to 6 while BDS7 and BDS8 are reproduction Sprite chassis. BDS3 is distinctive having no body pads on the top frame face. On these frames dummy rivets are used in conjunction with compensating welding.

The steel plate used on some reproduction chassis frames is much thinner than the $1/8^{th}$ standard and some box sections appear created with more folding

A system of publicly numbering these reproductions for identification purposes is much to be commended. Others clubs have used such a method.

185

One example of a copy of an Imp

*Based on a 1936 Riley Saloon and built with great attention to detail
completed in 2003*

This one is genuine!

Roberto Ravetta thoroughly at home, rallying in the Dolomite peaks, see page 160

Appendix 1 The Basic Specification of the Riley Imp*

- Ladder frame chassis, with tubular cross bracing rivetted to outer faces, fully boxed with diagonal open channel sections
- 4 Cyl 1087 cc, 60.3 x 95.2mm, Hemispherical cylinder head with reduced hemisphere from standard, inclined valves
- Valve clearances 2-3''' hot, firing order 1243.
- Thermo siphon cooling, fan assisted driven from exhaust camshaft pulley
- External oil feed to upper engine areas
- Crankshaft solid machined billet, main bearings 1 ½" front and rear, Journals 1 $^{11}/_{16}$"
- Scintilla magneto or coil and distributor ignition,
- Twin SU Carbs 1", or twin Zenith 30mm
- Twin Exhaust form camshafts (inlet gear advanced one tooth)
- 45 bhp @ 5,000rpm, variable.
- 4 speed epicyclic gearbox 'Preselecta' ENV Wilson Patent, type 75 HR
- First or Second type centrifugal clutch
- Torque Tube transmission driving a 5.25 : 1 semi-floating rear axle
- Semi elliptic (gaitered) springs and Hartford friction shock absorbers
- 12 gallon fuel tank. (63 litres)
- Braking by single cable system through a central compensator, 13" (external dia) bi metal drums
- Steering by worm and wheel
- Wheels 19" tyres 4.50 x 19" at 34 psi
- Twin 6 volt batteries mounted behind seat squab
- Rotax Dynamo driven from front of crankshaft, adjustable 3rd brush, to give constant charge rate.
- Dashboard $^{5}/_{8}$" inch ply painted or lacquered
- Single seat squab with 'float-on-air' seat cushions
- Oil pressure 40 – 60 psi at road speeds, supplied by double plunger pump
- Water temperature 90° C.
- Maximum speed, 80 mph @ 5000rpm
- Kerb weight 17cwt , (1904 lbs or 863 kilos)
- Weight distribution 49% front, 51% rear.
- Wheelbase 7'6", track 3' 11½" , (2.285m x 1.21m)

*Specifications for the Ulster Imp differ in certain points. See p.15ff and listings.

APPENDIX 2. Riley Imps in Chassis Number Order

* Alterations made

Chassis No	Orig Reg'n No	1st Regn	Orig Eng No	Other Reg'n	Gearbox / ENV box No	Rear Axle No
0	KV 5086	33 show car?				
6024449	KV 8025	7.3.34	40106		ENV	
6024450	KV8026	7.3.34	47676			
6024755	AYK 597	30.4.34	24755		ENV	
6024757	KV 8932	15.5.34	24757		S/3rd *	
6024758	KV8933	15.5.34	24758		ENV	
6024867	KV 9475	1.6.34	41174		ENV	
6024868	KV 9476	1.6.34	41176		4233	
6024870	KV9550	11.6.34				
6024981		4.7.34				
6024990	ES 176				S/3 RD*	
6024992	ADU162	27.7.34	41178		S/3RD *	25620
6025034	ADU 300	18.8.34	41192		ENV	
6025035	ADU 301	18.8.34	41196		ENV	
6025036	ADU 303	22.8.34	41184		2424	
6025037	AVR 718	25.8.34	41186		4237	
6025038	ADU 302	18.8.34	41188		S/3RD '	
6025044	ADU 801	22.9.34	53938	OSU163	S/3RD*	53958
6025048	GYM 958	5.8.34	60462*		A/H *	
6025075	US 8803	27.11.34	54288	RLY9	ENV	
6025085	GRF 899					
6025144	AVU 808	20.10.34	54350		ENV	
6025145	AOJ 431	3.11.34	54346		ENV	
6025146	BGP 530	14.11.34	54340		ENV A/H*	24813
6025217	NKD 494	'1935	54482		ENV	
6025218	BOL734	11.1.36	54342	SNM517	ENV	
6025259	CPA 101	1.11.34	54344*		ENV	
6025339	WS 2374	18.12.34	54348		AH	
6025340	AXJ 993	13.12.34	54476	341MP	ENV	
6025410	AAD 556	'1934	47250*		ENV	

188

6025441	BGW 119	12.11.34	54472		ENV	
6025442	BLN 196	17.11.34	54360		1045	
6025443	BLK387	11.34	54484		ENV	
6025444	AHP 542	10.12.34	54354		ENV	
6025491	AUB 920	14.12.34	54358		S/3RD *	
6025492	ALJ 454	1.12.34	352956	SAA27	ENV	
6025493	BTW 763	8.12.34	54422		R 1930HR	24810
6025503	KVT208vl	(12/4)*		69AGO	A/S P/S	
6025506	JK 4309				ENV	
6025507	OW 6276	8.2.35	54368		AH	
6025510	AUG 865	1.2.35	55112*		ENV 75	
6025511	ATT 392	1.1.35	54424		ENV 75	25341
6025512	BHY 327	7.10.35	54824		1625	
6025513	WD 8853	19.1.35	55144		ENV	
6025517	CME412	1935	55110		ENV	
6025973	WS650	28.6.34				
6026098	KV8454	29.3.34	48892			
6026133	AHP545	17.12.34	54898		ENV -S 3rd*	
6027230	GC 2675		197156*		AH	25344
6027305	AON 434	20.2.35	55518*		ENV	
6027310	JM 4370	'1935	55508		ENV	
6027324	X 7275	1.4.35	55500		ENV	
6027335	O22 (Aust)		37-5724*	WXW988	ENV*	
6027351	CXU 569	14.7.36	55520		ENV	
6027359	OW 7859	7.11.35	55514		MANUAL	
6027360	BRR222a	1935	55785*	DSL 721	ENV	
6027369	JK 4454	13.3.35	55804		ENV R2032HR	25720
6027370	AJH 531	6.4.35	55844*		S/3RD	
6027405	BUW904	1.3.35	55842*		1986 HR	
6027413	BVR 15	30.3.35	55890		ENV	
6027414	VH 7503	11.3.35	55892		ENV	
6027421	ARW 491	14.3.35	55900	400MPA	ENV	
6027430	BNW 51	1935	55902		ENV 75	
6027431	JV 3506	30.3.35	55904		ENV	

189

6027432	BXL550	27.3.35	55912		ENV	
6027433	RR076	'1935	55910	KRH182	ENV	
6027438	APT 590	14.4.35	55938		ENV	25600
6027439	BYY 575	8.8.35	55936		R2001HR	25798
6027447	BYK 947	11.7.35	55950		AH now ENV	
6027462	BXM 820	8.4.35	55960		1988HR	
6027477	892 RMC	'1958		ADU301**	S/3 now ENV	
6027484	BXO 32	20.5.35	56014		ENV	
6027493	BAU 519	18.4.35	56022		R2018HR	
6027496	WG 3688	7.5.35	56020		R2019HR	
6027497	ARO 451	26.6.35	56042		ENV	
6027562	438855*	1935	54694*		AH *	
6027563	GUP 385		56348	IMP934	2023 HR	
6027627	BXV 671	1935	56312		ENV	
6027633	BYY 909		56316		R1997HR	
6027638	BXO31	20.5.35	62722*		R1989HR	
6027664			56404*			
6027665	O 11	11.6.35	12315*	EGS 981	A/H	
6027667	AUO347		56406		ENV	
6027668	CUU285	28.3.35	56416	MJ88	ENV	
6027673	DMP 520	1.4.36	56442		ENV	
6027674	FV 6310	31.7.35	56412		ENV	
6027675	CLD 597	1.3.36	56450		ENV	
6027676	CNW 213	14.8.35	56408*			
6027677	JK 4949	21.8.35	56420		R 24024HR	M26035
6027678	BRA763	29.6.35	56430	TSJ731	ENV	
6027679	BYV 466	23.8.35	56432		R2006HR	
6027680	SSV336*		(12/4*)		P/S	
6027681	AKV 443	12.9.35	56434		S/3rd	M26028
6027682	512 JTU *	'1935	50984		ENV 75	
6027683	CMV 91	20.9.35	56420*			
6027685	AKV 216	1.8.35	56448		R1991HR	M26034
6027686			56452*		ENV	
6027752	ZZ660*		(12/4)		ENV	

APPENDIX 3, Registration Numbers in Alphabetical Order for reference, including variations.

* Alterations made   **See also 892 RMC/ 6027477and page 184

Orig Reg No	Chassis No	Date Regn	Engine no	Other Reg Nos
341MP	6025340	13.12.34	54476	AXJ993
400MPA	6027421	14.3.35	55900	ARW491
438855*	6027562	1935	54694*	
512JTU *	6027682	1935	50984	
69AGO*	6025503		6,-12/4*	KVT208v
892 RMC	6027477	1958		ADU301**
AAD 556	6025410	1934	47250*	
ADU162	6024992	27.7.34	41178	
ADU 300	6025034	18.8.34	41192	
ADU 301	6025035	18.8.34	41196	
ADU301**	6027477**	1958		892RMC
ADU 302	6025038	18.8.34	41188	
ADU 303	6025036	22.8.34	41184	
ADU 801	6025044	22.9.34	53938	OSU163
AHP 542	6025444	10.12.34	54354	
AHP545	6026133	17.12.34	54898	
AJH 531	6027370	6.4.35	55844*	
AKV 216	6027685	1.8.35	56448	
AKV 443	6027681	12.9.35	56434	
ALJ 454	6025492	1.12.34	352956	SAA27
AOJ 431	6025145	3.11.34	54346	
AON 434	6027305	20.2.35	353094	
APT 590	6027438	14.4.35	55938	
APU 200	Works Regn			
ARO 451	6027497	26.6.35	56042	
ARW 491	6027421	14.3.35	55900	400MPA
ATT 392	6025511	1.1.35	54424	
AUB 920	6025491	14.12.34	54358	
AUG 865	6025510	1.2.35	55112*	
AUO 347	6027667		56406	

AVR 718	6025037	25.8.34	41186	
AVU 808	6025144	20.10.34	54350	
AXJ 993	6025340	13.12.34	54476	341MP
AYK 597	6024755	30.4.34	24755	
BAU 519	6027493	18.4.35	56022	
BGP 530	6025146	14.11.34	54340	
BGW 119	6025441	12.11.34	54472	
BHY 327	6025512	7.10.35	54824	
BLD 733	(M.Royce)	1934		
BLK387	6025443	11.34	54484	
BLL170	(Bira)	1934		
BLN 196	6025442	17.11.34	54360	
BNW 51	6027430	1935	55902	
BOL734	6025218	11.1.36	54342	SNM517
BPL 1	(1935 RAC)			
BRA763	6027678	29.6.35	56430	TSJ731
BRR222a	6027360	1935	55785*	DSL 721
BTW 763	6025493	8.12.34	54422	
BUW904	6027405	1.3.35	55842*	
BVR 15	6027413	30.3.35	55890	
BXL550	6027432	27.3.35	55912	
BXM 820	6027462	8.4.35	55960	
BXO31	6027638	20.5.35	62722*	
BXO 32	6027484	20.5.35	56014	
BXV 671	6027627	1935	56312	
BYK 947	6027447	11.7.35	55950	
BYV 466	6027679	23.8.35	56432	
BYY 575	6027439	8.8.35	55936	
BYY 909	6027633		56316	
CGH 353	(B.A.Leigh)			
CGH 400	(J.B.Ashton)			
CLD 597	6027675	1.3.36	56450	
CME412	6025517	1935	55110	
CMV 511	(UVCC)			

CMV 91	6027683	20.9.35	47252*	
CNW 213	6027676	14.8.35	56408*	
CPA 101	6025259	1.11.34	54344*	
CSU750	6025075	27.11.34		US8803
CUN272	6025503		6, -12/4	69AGO
CUU285	6027668	28.3.35	56416	MJ88
CXU 89		5.36		
CXU 569	6027351	14.7.36	55520	
DMP 520	6027673	1.4.36	56442	
DSL 721	6027360	1935	55785	BRR222a
EGS381	6027665	11.6.35	12315*	O 11
ES 176	6024990			
FV 6310	6027674	31.7.35	56412	
GC 2675	6027230		197156*	
GRF 899	6025085			
GUP 385	6027563		56348	IMP034
GX 731			55510	
GYM 958	6025048	5.8.34	60462*	
IMP934	6027563		56348	GUP385
JK 4309	6025506			
JK 4454	6027369	13.3.35	55804	
JK 4949	6027677	21.8.35	56420	
JM 4370	6027310	'1935	55508	
JV 3506	6027431	30.3.35	55904	
KRH 182	6027433	1935	55910	RR076
KV 5086	0	33 show car?		
KV 8025	6024449	7.3.34	40106	
KV8026	6024450	7.3.34	47676	
KV8454	6026098	29.3.34	48892	
KV 8932	6024757	15.5.34	24757	
KV8933	6024758	15.5.34	24758	
KV 9475	6024867	1.6.34	41174	
KV 9476	6024868	1.6.34	41176	
KV9550	6024870	11.6.34		

KVT208vl	6025503		6, -12/4*	69AGO
LRO797	(D.Millar)			
MJ88	6027668	28.3.35	56416	CUU285
NKD 494	6025217	'1935	54482	
O11 (Aust)	6027665	11.6.35	12315*	EGS381
O22 (Aust)	6027335		37-5724*	WXW988
OSU163	6025044	22.9.34	53938	ADU801
OW5506	(Dobbs)			
OW 6276	6025507	8.2.35	54368	
OW 7859	6027359	7.11.35	55514	
R88	6027668	28.3.35	56416	CUU285
RLY9	6025075	27.11.34	54288	US8803
RR076	6027433	'1935	55910	KVT182
SAA27	6025492	1.12.34	352956	ALJ454
SNM517	6025218	11.1.35	54342	BOL734
SSV336*	6027680		(12/4*)	K35 336
TSJ731	6027678	29.6.35	56430	BRA763
UE 255	6027433	1935	55910	RR076
US 8803	6025075	27.11.34	54288	RLY9
VH 7503	6027414	11.3.35	55892	
WD 8853	6025513	19.1.35	55144	
WG 3688	6027496	7.5.35	56020	
WN 4070		Late 34		
WS 2374	6025339	18.12.34	54348	
WS650	6025973	28.6.34		
WXW988	6027335		37-5724*	
X 7275	6027324	1.4.35	55500	
XNU 298				
YX 1967	(Densham)			
ZZ 660*	6027752		(12/4)	
	6024981	4.7.34		
	6027664		56404*	
	6027686		56452*	

194

INDEX

196

198

199

Puzzle Picture

About the only car to worry the pre-war blown racing cars was the Riley, when given one carburetter per cylinder, in four-cylinder and six-cylinder forms.

It looks like an Ulster Imp, but has an internal exhaust and lacks the cross member immediately in front of the radiator, here in a hot climate, but Z2178 remains a mystery.

200

Tailpieces

Mike Hawthorn in his Ulster Imp ©LAT Photographic

Another shot of the lost car BPL1 on the 1935 RAC rally ©LAT Photographic

ADU303 post war at Lourenco Marques – photo from Rodney Green